God can create
roa [illegible] e
see [illegible] tacles

A Special Gift

To

From

Date

POWERFUL *Moments with God*

Kay Arthur

HARVEST HOUSE PUBLISHERS

EUGENE, OREGON

These excerpts were originally published as an inspirational calender under the title *His Imprint, My Expression* by Kay Arthur.

Cover by Koechel Peterson & Associates, Minneapolis, MN.

POWERFUL MOMENTS WITH GOD

Published by Harvest House Publishers

Eugene, Oregon 97402 www.harvesthousepublishers.com

ISBN 978-0-7369-2361-3

Printed in China

09 10 11 12 13 14 15 / RDS-SK / 10 9 8 7 6 5 4 3 2

Powerful Moments with God

❧ I ❧

By My Spirit

"Not by might nor by power…
but by My Spirit," says the LORD *of hosts.*

ZECHARIAH 4:6

In each of us there is a longing for the spiritual. Because we are not simply body and soul, there's an awareness, a sense of need for something, someone beyond ourselves. Many times we become aware of this when we finally come up against something we cannot control. But what we cannot do, God can—by His Spirit.

REFLECTIONS

....

....

....

....

....

❧ 2 ❧

Always There for You

When Thou didst say, "Seek My face," my heart said to Thee, "Thy face, O LORD, I shall seek."

PSALM 27:8

Beloved, have you ever longed for someone to take you by the hand and walk you safely through the traumas of life? There is One who is always there to listen…to guide…to mark your life with the imprint of His own. This year, God wants to speak to your heart through His Word and by His Spirit. Will you put your hand in His in child-like trust and say with me, "Yes, Lord…"?

REFLECTIONS

....

....

....

....

....

✣ 3 ✣

God Chose Us!

He chose us in Him before the foundation of the world.

Ephesians 1:4

Why was I born? What is the purpose of my life? Have you ever asked yourself these questions? I was considering them just the other day. As I did, my mind went to this amazing truth: Even before God created the heavens and the earth, He knew you and me, *and He chose us!* You and I were born because it was God's good pleasure!

REFLECTIONS

....

....

....

....

....

4

Your Life Has a Purpose

For we are His workmanship, created in Christ Jesus for good works, which God prepared beforehand, that we should walk in them.

Ephesians 2:10

Do you realize how absolutely precious you are to God? If you think you aren't or feel differently, you have embraced a lie. You are of value. Your life is significant. It has a purpose. A specific purpose. Not only were you chosen before the world's foundation but God also prepared a plan for your life alone—and neither man nor the devil can destroy that plan.

REFLECTIONS

⚜ 5 ⚜

Dependent on God Alone

In love He predestined us to adoption…
through Jesus Christ to Himself, according to
the kind intention of His will.

Ephesians 1:4,5

Can I share a secret with you, precious one? Your worth and purpose do not depend on what you have done, or what has been done to you or where you have been, even if you have been to the very precipice of hell. Your worth and purpose depend on God and God alone—His will, His calling, His choosing, His love.

REFLECTIONS

....

....

....

....

....

6

God's Love for You

In this is love, not that we loved God,
but that He loved us and sent His Son to be
the propitiation for our sins.

1 JOHN 4:10

Have you begun to grasp the breadth, length, height, and depth of God's love for you? When you were a sinner, ungodly, and without hope, God loved you, pursued you, and wooed you. And He did not let go until you gave in to His desire to be your Father, your Lord, your Redeemer. That is what you are worth to Him.

REFLECTIONS

....

....

....

....

....

❧ 7 ❧

Choose to Believe God

The sum of Thy word is truth.

Psalm 119:160

Do you sometimes find yourself lost in the maze of the enemy's lies? Your peace, soundness of mind, and effectiveness all depend on what you believe—and *whom* you believe. It does not matter what you feel, think, or hear. If it does not agree with the Word of God, it is a lie. Don't miss knowing your worth and purpose by believing lies of men or the musings of your mind. Choose to believe God.

REFLECTIONS

June 24, 2010

8

In the Light of God's Grace

I count all things to be loss in view of
the surpassing value of knowing Christ Jesus
my Lord...and count them but rubbish in
order that I may gain Christ.

PHILIPPIANS 3:8

Everything you are going through, all that you are dealing with, has one ultimate purpose: that you may know the love of God and live in the light of His extravagant and more-than-adequate grace. You were born for an intimate relationship with God. That is the purpose of your existence. And when you discover that, you'll experience an abiding contentment.

REFLECTIONS

....

....

....

....

....

❧ 9 ❧

Learning to Recognize God's Voice

And your ears will hear a word behind you,
"This is the way, walk in it," whenever you
turn to the right or to the left.

Isaiah 30:21

Do you want an intimate relationship with God? If so, you must consistently and faithfully set aside time so your heavenly Father can communicate with you through His Word and by His Spirit. Talk with Him in prayer. Put yourself in a position for God to meet with you, and everything else will fall into perspective. You will learn to recognize His voice.

REFLECTIONS

....

....

....

....

....

❧ 10 ❧

Focus on God

For to me, to live is Christ, and to die is gain.

PHILIPPIANS 1:21

Paul wrote these words while a prisoner of Rome. His epistle has come to be known as a letter of joy. Why? How? Both questions are answered in two words, one Person: Jesus Christ. Paul's focus was on Jesus, not on his own life or his circumstances. Where is your focus today? Joy comes when it is Jesus first, others second...then you. And if to live is Christ, there's always joy.

REFLECTIONS

❧ 11 ❧

Please God Alone

Whom have I in heaven but Thee?
And besides Thee, I desire nothing on earth.

Psalm 73:25

When God is our focus, everything else—including self—has to take a back seat. He is the only One we have to please. Isn't that refreshing? We don't have to be afraid that such an attitude will make us hard or unloving or uncaring. What God works out in our lives will reflect His character, His likeness...His imprint.

REFLECTIONS

....

....

....

....

....

❧ 12 ❧

Seek God's Favor

For am I now seeking the favor of men,
or of God? Or am I striving to please men?
If I were still trying to please men, I would not
be a bond-servant of Christ.

GALATIANS 1:10

When we are set free from the bondage of pleasing others and of pleasing ourselves (and trying to always please others is bondage) and when we are free from currying others' favor and others' approval—then no one will be able to make us miserable or dissatisfied. If we know we have pleased God, contentment will be our consolation, for what pleases God will please us.

REFLECTIONS

....

....

....

....

....

❧ 13 ❧

God Holds the Key

The Lord *of hosts has sworn saying, "Surely, just as I have intended so it has happened, and just as I have planned so it will stand."*

Isaiah 14:24

If you are frustrated, Beloved, because something has gone wrong—you did the wrong thing, made the wrong decision—remember God is even sovereign over the contingencies of life. He is the great redeemer, and He can even redeem this one! Confess what you did wrong. He knows your weakness—trust Him and go forward in faith. You will learn, and you will be more conformed to His image. He promises.

REFLECTIONS

....

....

....

....

....

14

Live by God's Power

For it is God who is at work in you, both to will and to work for His good pleasure.

Philippians 2:13

Do you want to live a life that pleases God? He has given you the means to do so, Beloved, because in the wonderful mystery of salvation, Christ dwells in you. You are complete in Him. He will meet you right where you are. He does not expect you to have the talents, gifts, or personality of others. You are His unique creation. Now you can live by *His* power, which will work in you and lead you into the good works He has ordained for you.

REFLECTIONS

....

....

....

....

....

One Day at a Time

Commit your way to the LORD,
trust also in Him, and He will do it.

PSALM 37:5

O Beloved, the will of God is simply that you submit yourself to Him each day and say, "Father, Your will for today is mine. Your pleasure for today is mine. Your work for today is mine." Take one day at a time. *"Tomorrow will care for itself"* (Matthew 6:34). And remember, He is God over all your tomorrows.

REFLECTIONS

....

....

....

....

....

16

His Grace Is Sufficient

Remember, O LORD, Thy compassion and Thy loving kindnesses, for they have been from of old.

PSALM 25:6

When you've failed, do you wonder how things could ever be the same between you and God? Don't you know, precious one, that you belong to the God of all grace? *Grace is the birthright of every child of God.* Grace is there to preserve you in the darkest night of your failures. His grace is sufficient for all your sin, for all your inadequacy, for all your powerlessness.

REFLECTIONS

17

Unmerited Favor

For by grace you have been saved through faith; and that not of yourselves, it is the gift of God.

EPHESIANS 2:8

Grace is unmerited favor bestowed on us at the moment of our salvation. The kingdom of heaven is reserved for those who become as little children, for those who look to their Father in loving confidence for every benefit, whether it be for the pardon so freely given or for the strength and power to do His will.

REFLECTIONS

....

....

....

....

....

18

The Lord Is Merciful

Behold, we count those blessed who endured. You have heard of the endurance of Job and have seen the outcome of the Lord's dealings, that the Lord is full of compassion and is merciful.

JAMES 5:11

Grace calls you to get up, to throw off your blanket of hopelessness, and to move on through life in faith. And what grace calls you to, grace provides. Grace is power.

REFLECTIONS

....

....

....

....

....

❧ 19 ❧

Grace upon Grace

For of His fulness we have all received,
and grace upon grace.

John 1:16

O Beloved, how often we seek to live in our own strength and to approach God on our own merit rather than on His grace! We fail to appropriate His grace, which is there to cover our failure and to save us from despair.

REFLECTIONS

....

....

....

....

....

20

God's Grace

And He has said to me, "My grace is sufficient for you, for power is perfected in weakness." Most gladly, therefore, I will rather boast about my weaknesses, that the power of Christ may dwell in me.

2 CORINTHIANS 12:9

We will never cease to need our Father—His wisdom, direction, help, and support. We will never outgrow Him. We will always need His grace. And His grace will never fail. It is not a well that will run dry, but it is an ocean whose depths you can never plumb.

REFLECTIONS

....

....

....

....

....

❧ 21 ❧

Grace Saves Us

But one thing I do: forgetting what lies behind and reaching forward to what lies ahead, I press on toward the goal for the prize of the upward call of God in Christ Jesus.

Philippians 3:13,14

The same grace that saves us is the grace that keeps us. It is not just grace to cover sin, it is grace more than sufficient to overcome *every* sin, *every* weakness. Grace enables us to live as more than conquerors day in and day out, no matter what. There's always grace to begin anew.

REFLECTIONS

....

....

....

....

....

Are You Living in Overdrive?

About midnight Paul and Silas were praying and singing hymns of praise to God.

ACTS 16:25

Are you living in overdrive? Life is filled with pressure—pressure to be, pressure to do, pressure to perform, pressure to produce. How can we release the pressures of the accelerated pace of our earthly life so that it doesn't break us? What we hear from the jail cell where Paul and Silas were imprisoned gives us a clue.

REFLECTIONS

23

Worship Through Music

Yet Thou art holy.

Psalm 22:3

A vital key to releasing the pressures of life is to worship through music. When we worship our Lord and our God in song, we become even more aware of His presence. The tension begins to unravel; the tautness eases; anxieties become meaningless, for we are reminded that He is there—our *Jehovah Shammah,* our all-sufficient, sovereign God.

REFLECTIONS

....

....

....

....

....

Worship God in Song

I will sing a new song to Thee, O God; upon a harp of ten strings I will sing praises to Thee.

Psalm 144:9

Do you begin your day in song? Try putting your CD player in your bathroom or bedroom. Play worship music or listen to Scripture while you're dressing. Sing in the shower. Play music while you do housework or drive to work. You'll find that the words will be engraved on the tablets of you heart and become an everpresent song on your lips.

REFLECTIONS

....

....

....

....

....

25

Songs of Deliverance

Thou art my hiding place;
Thou dost preserve me from trouble; Thou dost surround me with songs of deliverance.

PSALM 32:7

Singing spiritual songs and making melody in your heart is God's way of delivering you from the stresses of the world. The more you enter into His courts with praise and into His gates with thanksgiving, the less you will feel the pressure of daily life.

REFLECTIONS

....

....

....

....

....

26

Joy...No Matter What!

But the fruit of the Spirit is love, joy, peace, patience, kindness, goodness, faithfulness, gentleness, self-control; against such things there is no law.

GALATIANS 5:22,23

Did you know that you can have joy, Beloved? Joy...a deep, abiding, overriding joy no matter what! It's part of the wellspring of the Spirit for all who will draw from His riches. God's Word assures us that "joy no matter what" can become a reality for us who would grasp this truth and live by the Spirit.

REFLECTIONS

....

....

....

....

....

❧ 27 ❧

Complete Joy

If therefore there is any encouragement in Christ... make my joy complete by being of the same mind, maintaining the same love, united in spirit, intent on one purpose.

PHILIPPIANS 2:1,2

The key to having "joy no matter what" is found in the person of Jesus Christ and in an attitude that is submissive to His will. The apostle Paul's joy did not center on freedom from prison (and prisons take many forms, don't they?). Rather, his joy was wrapped up in the person and promises of Christ.

REFLECTIONS

....

....

....

....

....

28

God's Will

With all boldness, Christ shall even now,
as always, be exalted in my body,
whether by life or by death. For to me,
to live is Christ, and to die is gain.

Philippians 1:20,21

It did not matter to Paul whether he was locked up or free. Whatever God wanted to do with the apostle Paul was all right, for Paul's heart and mind were set on one thing: God's will for him. Paul knew that God, not man, held the keys to his prison doors.

REFLECTIONS

❧ 29 ❧

The Perfect Result

Consider it all joy...when you encounter various trials, knowing that the testing of your faith produces endurance. And let endurance have its perfect result, that you may be perfect and complete, lacking in nothing.

JAMES 1:2-4

Dear friend, whatever you are enduring now—or whatever comes your way in the future—it is not without purpose in the sovereignty of God. And it is for that reason, Beloved, that you can have that inward sense of joy. God promises that it will not destroy you—rather, over time it will be the making of you.

REFLECTIONS

....

....

....

....

....

❧ 30 ❧

Claim Your Joy

Now I want you to know, brethren,
that my circumstances have turned out for
the greater progress of the gospel.

PHILIPPIANS 1:12

Have people, things, or circumstances robbed you of your joy? Pray through Philippians 1, substituting your circumstances for Paul's. Make Paul's desire yours. Practice having his mind-set; claim the joy that will be yours. And know this: Your joy, in spite of imprisonment, will be used by God to reach others.

REFLECTIONS

....

....

....

....

....

❧ 31 ❧

Take God at His Word

And without faith it is impossible to please Him, for he who comes to God must believe that He is, and that He is a rewarder of those who seek Him.

HEBREWS 11:6

Walking in faith brings you to the Word of God, the Balm of Gilead. There you will be healed, cleansed, fed, nurtured, equipped, matured...and hear God's "well done" because you have taken Him at His Word. Faith always pleases our God.

REFLECTIONS

❧ 32 ❧

Handling the Memories of Failure

For if He causes grief, then He will have compassion according to His abundant loving kindness. For He does not afflict willingly, or grieve the sons of men. To crush under His feet....

LAMENTATIONS 3:32-34

Do your failures loom like a dark cloud? Do you find yourself remembering times when you weren't all you should have been, all you could have been? I understand. Such thoughts can be emotionally draining. Turn to the book of Lamentations, and there you'll find hope for handling those haunting failures.

REFLECTIONS

....

....

....

....

....

❧ 33 ❧

A God of Love

The LORD'S lovingkindnesses indeed never cease, for His compassions never fail. They are new every morning; great is Thy faithfulness.

LAMENTATIONS 3:22,23

God is a God of unconditional, unremitting love, a love that corrects and chastens but never ceases. Therefore, when we fail Him our failures never alter or sway who God is. You can know for a certainty that His compassions are new every morning and His mercies fail not. Even when we are faithless He abides faithful.

REFLECTIONS

....

....

....

....

....

34

Teach Me, Lord

*Before I was afflicted I went astray,
but now I keep Thy word. Thou art good
and doest good: teach me Thy statutes.*

Psalm 119:67, 68

Let failure be your teacher, not your executioner.

REFLECTIONS

....

....

....

....

....

❧ 35 ❧

Handling Failure

"The Lord *is my portion," says my soul,*
"Therefore I have hope in Him."

Lamentations 3:24

Listen to the infallible Word of God! Hang on to all the promises of God—bring them up against your feelings. Live according to His Word, and eventually you'll find you can handle failure and even benefit yourself and others by dealing with it honestly before God.

REFLECTIONS

....

....

....

....

....

36

When Peace Is Gone

Finally, brethren, whatever is true...
whatever is right, whatever is pure...
let your mind dwell on these things.

PHILIPPIANS 4:8

Have you ever been doing just great, and then someone says something or you remember an incident from the past and suddenly your peace is gone? A cloud of depression begins to overshadow the contentment you felt just moments ago. You must do what God says, Beloved—put away such thoughts. The past is past.

REFLECTIONS

Changing Thoughts

We are taking every thought captive to the obedience of Christ.

2 Corinthians 10:5

One Sunday our son David came to say goodbye before returning to college. I'd been taking a nap, so I prayed for him and then rolled over to catch another "forty winks." Suddenly the "what ifs" attacked. Had I been the mother I should have been? Had I adequately prepared my son for life? My peace was gone. I allowed myself to anticipate calamity rather than entrust his future to my sovereign God. What will you do when the "what ifs" attack?

REFLECTIONS

❧ 38 ❧

Mental Warfare

...taking up the shield of faith with which you will be able to extinguish all the flaming missiles of the evil one.

Ephesians 6:16

Where do thoughts of inadequacy and fear come from? So often we forget that we are in warfare and that Satan's target is our mind. He disguises himself, of course! He doesn't want us to think he has anything at all to do with our thought process. Yet he does. And that is why we are to *take up the shield of faith.*

REFLECTIONS

....

....

....

....

....

❧ 39 ❧

Walk by Faith

God causes all things to work together for good to those who love God, to those who are called according to His purpose.

Romans 8:28

How can we be victorious in mental warfare? First, when unlovely, untrue thoughts invade our minds, we must choose to bring every one of them captive to the obedience of Jesus Christ. Then we must walk by faith rather than by our feelings, thoughts, and self-evaluations. No matter what our past, God's Word holds this sure promise.

REFLECTIONS

....

....

....

....

....

❧ 40 ❧

Cry to God

I will cry to God Most High, to God who accomplishes all things for me.

Psalm 57:2

Gracious and holy Father, give me wisdom to perceive You; intelligence to fathom You; patience to wait for You; eyes to behold You; a heart to meditate upon You; and a life to proclaim You, through the power of the Spirit of Jesus Christ, our Lord.

—*Benedict*

REFLECTIONS

....

....

....

....

....

❧ 41 ❧

Misery Will Slip Away

Those who love Thy law have great peace,
and nothing causes them to stumble.

Psalm 119:165

The wonderful benefit of living in a way that pleases God is that if you make the will of God your focus day by day, if you seek to please Him alone, you'll find yourself satisfied with life. Misery will slip away like a whipped puppy with its tail between its legs.

REFLECTIONS

....

....

....

....

....

God's Unconditional Love

I will call those who were not My people, "My people," and her who was not beloved, "beloved."

ROMANS 9:25

I remember the day my life was turned around by Jesus Christ. On July 16, I moved from a religion to a relationship. I saw my sin and my helplessness to change, and acknowledged that Jesus was God and had a right to rule my life. It was then that I was bathed in His unconditional love and experienced forgiveness of my numerous sins. When there was nothing lovely about me, God called me "beloved." If you have not experienced the same... do what I did. He wants you as His beloved.

REFLECTIONS

....

....

....

....

....

❧ 43 ❧

When You Question God's Love

For I am convinced that neither death, nor life, nor angels, nor principalities, nor things present, nor things to come, nor powers, nor height, nor depth, nor any other created thing, shall be able to separate us from the love of God, which is in Christ Jesus our Lord.

Romans 8:38,39

What a truth to cling to when we begin to doubt God's love...because of the severity of our pain, the enormity of our loss, the incongruity of the situation. The essence of God's being is love—He never separates Himself from that.

REFLECTIONS

....

....

....

....

....

44

Do You Lack Confidence in God?

And I said, "What shall I do, Lord?" And the Lord said to me, "…You will be told of all that has been appointed for you to do."

Acts 22:10

Dear friend, when you don't embrace in faith what God says about you, you'll find you lack confidence in God—in His unconditional love, in His help, in His desire to use you. Your attention turns to what's wrong in you. How much better to leave the pit of self-pity, shake the dust from your past, and move forward in His promises.

REFLECTIONS

....

....

....

....

....

❧ 45 ❧

No Excuses

...seeing that His divine power has granted to us everything pertaining to life and godliness, through the true knowledge of Him who called us by His own glory and excellence.

2 PETER 1:3

God has made every provision you need, as His child, to keep your heart pure. However, it is your responsibility to appropriate His provisions and live accordingly. No excuse will be accepted when you stand before Him!

REFLECTIONS

❧ 46 ❧

Forgiveness

But the lovingkindness of the LORD is from everlasting to everlasting on those who fear Him, and His righteousness to children's children, to those who keep His covenant, and who remember His precepts to do them.

PSALM 103:17,18

"In Christ" is a key phrase in the epistles. However, it may be that the enemy blinds you to this truth and whispers in your ear, "You're no good. You'll never amount to much." Beloved, if you are God's child, you are no longer a sinner. You are a saint (one set apart for God, sanctified). You have received forgiveness for all your sins—past, present, and future.

REFLECTIONS

....

....

....

....

....

❧ 47 ❧

A New Creature

Therefore from now on we recognize no man according to the flesh; even though we have known Christ according to the flesh, yet now we know Him thus no longer. Therefore if any man is in Christ, he is a new creature; the old things passed away; behold, new things have come.

2 Corinthians 5:16,17

If you are God's child, you are no longer bound to your past or to what you were. You are a brand new creature in Christ Jesus.

REFLECTIONS

....

....

....

....

....

48

Walk in Newness of Life

Therefore we have been buried with Him through baptism into death, in order that as Christ was raised from the dead through the glory of the Father, so we too might walk in newness of life.

Romans 6:4

As God's child you are no longer a slave to sin. As a servant of righteousness, you don't have to let sin rule in your body.

REFLECTIONS

❧ 49 ❧

Delivered from Darkness

For He delivered us from the domain of darkness, and transferred us to the kingdom of His beloved Son.

Colossians 1:13

As God's child, you are no longer part of the kingdom of darkness, but have been seated in heavenly places above all the power of the evil one and his demonic forces.

REFLECTIONS

....

....

....

....

....

❧ 50 ❧

Just As You Are

And because you are sons, God has sent forth the Spirit of His Son into our hearts, crying, "Abba! Father!"

GALATIANS 4:6

As God's child, you are no longer rejected but are accepted in the Beloved—just as you are—because God chose you for Himself before the foundation of the world. You have been adopted as God's dear child and are sealed by His Spirit, who guarantees that you will live with God forever (Ephesians 1:3-14).

REFLECTIONS

....

....

....

....

....

God Has Removed Our Transgressions

As far as the east is from the west, so far has He removed our transgressions from us.

Psalm 103:12

As a child of God, you no longer have to fear the consequences of your past.

REFLECTIONS

❧ 52 ❧

The Lord Is My Helper

He Himself has said, "I will never desert you, nor will I ever forsake you," so that we confidently say, "The Lord is my helper, I will not be afraid. What shall man do to me?"

HEBREWS 13:5,6

As God's child, you no longer have to fear being abandoned, left alone, or left without help.

REFLECTIONS

❧ 53 ❧

In the Lord's Hand

Since his days are determined, the number of his months is with Thee, and his limits Thou hast set so that he cannot pass.... In whose hand is the life of every living thing, and the breath of all mankind?

Job 14:5; 12:10

As a child of God, you no longer have to fear death, for you cannot die before your time. Jesus holds the keys to hell and death. When you die, you will be immediately absent from the body and present with the Lord (Revelation 1:18; 2 Corinthians 5:8,9).

REFLECTIONS

....

....

....

....

....

54

Draw Near with Confidence

Let us therefore draw near with confidence to the throne of grace, that we may receive mercy and may find grace to help in time of need.

Hebrews 4:16

As His child, you no longer need to fear approaching God. You can come boldly to His throne and find His mercy—unearned favor and help—in the time of your need.

REFLECTIONS

....

....

....

....

....

❧ 55 ❧

All Your Needs

And my God shall supply all your needs according to His riches in glory in Christ Jesus.

PHILIPPIANS 4:19

As God's child, you no longer are to fear not having exactly what you need...physically, emotionally, spiritually, materially. God promises to supply all of your needs through Christ Jesus your Lord.

REFLECTIONS

⁂ 56 ⁂

You Belong to Christ

And you belong to Christ;
and Christ belongs to God.

1 Corinthians 3:23

Why not read the New Testament epistles, beginning with Romans, where "in Christ" is a key phrase? Ask God to show you personally who you are in Christ Jesus and what is yours because you belong to Him. If you'll do this, your life will take on a whole new dimension.

REFLECTIONS

....

....

....

....

....

❧ 57 ❧

Believe!

What then shall we say to these things? If God is for us, who is against us? He who did not spare His own Son, but delivered Him up for us all, how will He not also with Him freely give us all things?

ROMANS 8:31,32

God loved you—just the way you were—and gave His Son for you. He put you in Jesus Christ and Jesus Christ in you. What more can God do? What more can He say? He's done it all in His Son. He's said it all in His Word. Now, you must do your part: Believe!

REFLECTIONS

....

....

....

....

....

58

Our God Is Merciful

Then the LORD passed by in front of him and proclaimed, "The LORD, the LORD God, compassionate and gracious, slow to anger, and abounding in lovingkindness and truth."

EXODUS 34:6

Our God is not an implacable, rigid, judgmental Father who can never be pleased and who delights to catch us in a fault. How grossly wrong this thinking is! He is merciful, loving, and gracious toward His children.

REFLECTIONS

....

....

....

....

....

❧ 59 ❧

Run to God

But it is still my consolation, and I rejoice in unsparing pain, that I have not denied the words of the Holy One.

Job 6:10

When trials come your way—as inevitably they will—do not run away. Run to your God and Father.

REFLECTIONS

....

....

....

....

....

What Is a Christian?

For all have sinned and fall short of the glory of God, being justified as a gift by His grace through the redemption which is in Christ Jesus.

ROMANS 3:23,24

Have you ever thought about what a Christian is? Christians are people who have shuddered at the awfulness of their sin. They have seen sin for what it is: willful rebellion against the rulership of God in their lives. And in turning from their sin, they have embraced God's only means of dealing with sin: Jesus.

REFLECTIONS

❧ 61 ❧

Stolen Joy

Set your mind on the things above, not on the things that are on earth.

Colossians 3:2

"Things" can rob you of your joy. I'll never forget the time I bought a pair of bed sheets on sale, and then couldn't find matching pillowcases. Imagine! I'd try to study or teach and all I could think about were sheets. Ridiculous? Yes. But don't you have your own story of how some insignificant "thing" stole your joy?

REFLECTIONS

62

Christlikeness

But whatever things were gain to me, those things I have counted as loss for the sake of Christ.

PHILIPPIANS 3:7

The apostle Paul knew that only one thing could or should be central to him. What was that? Christlikeness. So, he determined that he would develop a single mind by making Christ his goal. To do this, Paul literally had to count everything else as rubbish.

REFLECTIONS

63

More Like Jesus

For we who live are constantly being delivered over to death for Jesus' sake, that the life of Jesus also may be manifested in our mortal flesh.

2 Corinthians 4:11

When we stand before Him, one second in eternity will erase all care or thought of anything except whether or not we allowed the situations of life to make us more like Him. So remember, every situation that requires us to crucify our desires, our reactions, is an opportunity to let people see Jesus in us.

REFLECTIONS

....

....

....

....

....

Fixing Our Eyes on Jesus

Let us also lay aside every encumbrance...and let us run with endurance the race that is set before us, fixing our eyes on Jesus.

Hebrews 12:1,2

If I am going to run the race set before me, I must never take my eyes off the goal—and I must run in my lane. What God asks, does, or requires of others is not my business; it is His. I am to be faithful to His calling on my life. He's the one waiting with His reward at the finish line.

REFLECTIONS

65

Let It Go

But whatever things were gain to me, those things
I have counted as loss for the sake of Christ.

Philippians 3:7

When "things," even things that are cause for celebration or expectation, begin to rob you of His joy, take a careful look at the "thing" in the light of eternity. If it will hinder you from getting on with what God has for you, let it go.

REFLECTIONS

66

Take Every Thought Captive

We are destroying speculations and every lofty thing raised up against the knowledge of God, and we are taking every thought captive to the obedience of Christ.

2 Corinthians 10:5

When something robs you of your peace of mind, ask yourself if it is worth the energy you are expending on it. If not, then put it out of your mind in an act of discipline. Every time the thought of "it" returns, refuse it.

REFLECTIONS

67

A Steadfast Spirit

Create in me a clean heart, O God,
and renew a steadfast spirit within me.

PSALM 51:10

Can you change whatever is robbing you of joy? Turn it around? Rectify it? Live without it? If there is nothing you can do to change it, then be obedient, walk in faith, and forget those things which are behind and press on toward the prize of your high calling in Christ Jesus.

REFLECTIONS

68

Be Content

I have learned to be content in whatever circumstances I am.

Philippians 4:11

Yes, Beloved, circumstances can also rob us of our joy. The apostle Paul was well aware of this as he wrote to the believers at Philippi, for he himself was a prisoner of Rome. His circumstances were less than ideal! Yet Paul lived in peace and contentment despite his circumstances. How? Christ was his life. All he wanted was for Jesus to be exalted in his body, whether by life or by death.

REFLECTIONS

....

....

....

....

....

69

God Is Eternal

We look not at the things which are seen, but at the things which are not seen; for the things which are seen are temporal, but the things which are not seen are eternal.

2 Corinthians 4:18

Have you ever found yourself distracted—so busy pursuing earthly things, earthly pleasures that it has dulled your interest for the eternal? It's not worth it, Beloved, for the temporal is just that—temporary—and it can disappear in a moment. But the eternal will last forever.

REFLECTIONS

70

Rejoice!

Rejoice in the Lord always;
again I will say, rejoice!

Philippians 4:4

Do you want to know a sure way to have victory and peace in the midst of any situation? Rejoice! The minute you begin rejoicing, your circumstances cease to control you. The command to rejoice does not mean rejoicing in your circumstances; it means rejoicing in your Savior who is Lord over every circumstance.

REFLECTIONS

A Matter of Obedience

I, Nebuchadnezzar, raised my eyes toward heaven, and my reason returned to me, and I blessed the Most High and praised and honored Him who lives forever.... He does according to His will in the host of heaven and among the inhabitants of earth; and no one can ward off His hand or say to Him, "What hast Thou done?"

DANIEL 4:34,35

Are you in a predicament? You could not be where you are without the Lord's foreknowledge. God is sovereign: He rules over all—nothing happens without His permission. Rejoicing is a matter of obedience—an obedience that will start you on the road to peace and contentment.

REFLECTIONS

....

....

....

....

....

⚜ 72 ⚜

Live by Faith

I can do all things through
Him who strengthens me.

PHILIPPIANS 4:13

We are to live by faith, not feelings. To paraphrase Paul's words: "I can keep on bearing all things through Him who constantly infuses His strength into me." Christ's strength, His grace, His power are sufficient to enable us to endure whatever comes our way.

REFLECTIONS

....

....

....

....

....

❧ 73 ❧

Be Strong and Courageous!

Have I not commanded you? Be strong and courageous! Do not tremble or be dismayed, for the LORD *your God is with you wherever you go.*

JOSHUA 1:9

What does it mean to be strong and courageous? To be strong is to refuse to be weak—weak in trust, weak in conviction, weak in obedience. To be courageous is to step out in faith—to trust and obey, no matter what.

REFLECTIONS

....

....

....

....

....

❧ 74 ❧

Jesus Is Watching

Let your forbearing spirit [sweet reasonableness] be known to all men. The Lord is near.

PHILIPPIANS 4:5

O my friend, what do you do when you feel "out of sorts" with others? Let them have it? Or at least let them know it? Don't! Jesus is there watching, and He's sufficient.

REFLECTIONS

....

....

....

....

....

75

Rejoice, No Matter What!

Discipline yourself for the purpose of godliness.

I Timothy 4:7

No matter what our circumstances, we can rejoice and let our forbearing spirit be known to all, receiving from our Lord the power to do so and accepting that power in faith, remembering He is at hand!

REFLECTIONS

....

....

....

....

....

Anxious for Nothing

Be anxious for nothing, but in everything by prayer and supplication with thanksgiving let your requests be made known to God.

Philippians 4:6

The world will tell you that it is natural and normal to be anxious. Well, anxiety may be natural and normal for the world, but it is not to be part of a believer's lifestyle!

REFLECTIONS

....

....

....

....

....

❧ 77 ❧

Look First to God

Be anxious for nothing, but in everything by prayer and supplication with thanksgiving let your requests be made known to God.

PHILIPPIANS 4:6

The moment anxious thoughts invade your mind, go to the Lord in prayer. Look first to God. Rehearse His character, His promises, His works. Remember His names, His attributes, and how they apply to your situation. You will see the cause of your anxiety in a whole new light.

REFLECTIONS

....

....

....

....

....

❧ 78 ❧

Live by God's Word

Do not be anxious for tomorrow.

MATTHEW 6:34

Dear friend, don't be anxious in the midst of today, and don't become anxious thinking about tomorrow. God, who rules over today, rules over tomorrow. He neither slumbers nor sleeps so He's there at the stroke of midnight, ready to care for you.

REFLECTIONS

...

...

...

...

...

79

Trials

We are afflicted in every way, but not crushed; perplexed, but not despairing...For we who live are constantly being delivered over to death for Jesus' sake, that the life of Jesus also may be manifested in our mortal flesh.

2 CORINTHIANS 4:8,11

Yes, we are tempted on every hand. The world is appealing. To one degree or another, our lives will be filled with disappointments, discouragements, defeats, difficulties. God's Word calls these "trials." Yet God says that trials are for our good; they are intended to make us more like Jesus.

REFLECTIONS

....

....

....

....

....

80

Salvation

The wind blows where it wishes and you hear the sound of it, but do not know where it comes from and where it is going; so is everyone who is born of the Spirit.

John 3:8

Aren't you just awed at the mystery of salvation? One minute a person is lost, and the next minute he or she is saved! You don't see anything spectacular or mysterious taking place; and yet, all of a sudden, the person is a brand-new creature in Christ Jesus, indwelt by the Spirit of God because he has been born again.

REFLECTIONS

....

....

....

....

....

Thanksgiving

And the peace of God, which surpasses all comprehension, shall guard your hearts and your minds in Christ Jesus.

Philippians 4:7

The act of thanksgiving is a demonstration of the fact that you are going to trust, to believe God. Thanksgiving is where faith comes in. And what is the end result? Peace instead of anxiety.

REFLECTIONS

Lasting Fruit

Even so, every good tree bears good fruit;
but the bad tree bears bad fruit...So then,
you will know them by their fruits.

MATTHEW 7:17,20

How can you tell the professors—those who merely name the name of Christ—from the possessors—those who are truly indwelt by Him? According to the Word of God, true Christianity brings forth lasting fruit—the evidence of salvation. For the next few days we'll be doing some fruit inspecting!

REFLECTIONS

❧ 83 ❧

A Person's Walk

If we say that we have fellowship with Him and yet walk in the darkness, we lie and do not practice the truth.

1 John 1:6

The first fruit that gives evidence of a genuine faith is a person's walk. A Christian walks the way Jesus walked, ordering his or her behavior accordingly. Jesus is the light of the world. He did not walk in darkness—and neither can those who are His true followers.

REFLECTIONS

....

....

....

....

....

Habitual Sin

And you know that He appeared in order to take away sins; and in Him there is no sin. No one who abides in Him sins [present tense in the Greek; implying continuous or habitual action]; *no one who sins has seen Him or knows Him.*

1 John 3:5,6

A true Christian does not live in habitual sin. Oh, yes, we do commit singular acts of sin, but sin—a life lived independently of God—cannot be the habit of our lives!

REFLECTIONS

....

....

....

....

....

❧ 85 ❧

Continued Perseverence

They went out from us, but they were not really of us; for if they had been of us, they would have remained with us; but they went out, in order that it might be shown that they all are not of us.

1 John 2:19

Another evidence of genuine faith is continued perseverance. Can a person be saved and then turn away from what he or she once professed as clearly set forth in the Word of God? No. Mark it well, Beloved: True believers do not permanently stray from God.

REFLECTIONS

Love of Others

The one who says he is in the light and yet hates his brother is in the darkness until now.... We know that we have passed out of death into life, because we love the brethren.

1 JOHN 2:9; 3:14

A true Christian cannot help but love others. Love of others is evidence of a genuine faith. Because love is an attribute of God, and because a Christian is a person who is indwelt by God, then it is only logical that love would be a fruit that a child of God would bear!

REFLECTIONS

....

....

....

....

....

❧ 87 ❧

Overcomers

For whatever is born of God overcomes the world; and this is the victory that has overcome the world—our faith. And who is the one who overcomes the world, but he who believes that Jesus is the Son of God?

1 JOHN 5:4,5

Read Jesus' messages to the churches in Revelation 2–3. Look at the rewards given to overcomers and you'll see that true believers are overcomers. Because Christ is in us and because He, by the Holy Spirit, enables us to keep His commandments, we are able to overcome the world!

REFLECTIONS

....

....

....

....

....

88

God's Abiding Spirit

By this we know that we abide in Him and He in us, because He has given us of His Spirit.

1 John 4:13

Another evidence of genuine faith is the inward witness of the Spirit of God (Romans 8:14-16). If a person has the witness of the Spirit in his heart, he will also have all the other evidences of salvation. These manifestations of genuine Christianity will be evident to one degree or another throughout the Christian's sojourn here on earth.

REFLECTIONS

....

....

....

....

....

89

A Thirst for Righteousness

Blessed are those who hunger and thirst for righteousness, for they shall be satisfied.

MATTHEW 5:6

Once the Holy Spirit moves in a person's heart—convicting of sin, righteousness, and judgment—there is an awakening of a thirst for righteousness, a longing to be finished with sin and its awful harvest. Then, when in salvation the Holy Spirit takes up His residence within a child of God, the Spirit causes him to set his mind on the things of the Spirit (Romans 8:1-8).

REFLECTIONS

....

....

....

....

....

90

Hungry for God's Word

Now we have received, not the spirit of the world, but the Spirit who is from God, that we might know the things freely given to us by God.

1 CORINTHIANS 2:12

How can you tell the saved from the lost? The saved are hungry for His Word and His righteousness. This is the seventh evidence of genuine faith. It is the Spirit of God within us who not only gives us a hunger for God's Word, but also enables us to understand the things of God. The veil comes off when Christ comes in!

REFLECTIONS

....

....

....

....

....

❧ 91 ❧

Choose Jesus

I have been crucified with Christ…
And the life which I now live in the flesh I live
by faith in the Son of God, who loved me,
and delivered Himself up for me.

GALATIANS 2:20

Jesus Christ alone is to be my one desire—His life, not mine. I am to love Him above all else, above all others. And when choices are to be made, I am to choose Him above all others. After all, Jesus is Lord. He is God. He is to have preeminence in my life.

REFLECTIONS

92

Wait for the Lord

Wait for the LORD; be strong, and let your heart take courage; yes, wait for the LORD.

PSALM 27:14

Are you hanging on by your fingernails, dear one? If I didn't know what I know about God, I might tell you to call it quits and to get on with your life. But because God is who He is, because our times are in His hands, I have to tell you not to give up. Don't "get on with your life." Wait, wait, I say, for the Lord, for His direction, His solution. He's never late.

REFLECTIONS

❧ 93 ❧

Sit at His Feet

Martha, Martha, you are worried and bothered about so many things; but only a few things are necessary, really only one, for Mary has chosen the good part, which shall not be taken away from her.

Luke 10:41,42

How do you "wait for the Lord?" First you must learn to sit at His feet and take time to "listen to His words." Martha, who was eager to "do for the Lord," was distracted from Him by her preparations for the Lord—by her "much serving." This can easily become so true of us. It's noticeable when we start criticizing others and thinking the Lord doesn't care about us!

REFLECTIONS

....

....

....

....

....

❧ 94 ❧

The One Needful Thing

Cease striving [let go, relax] and
know that I am God.

Psalm 46:10

Beloved, sitting at Jesus' feet and listening to His Word is a choice. Some things will not get done. Some people will not understand. But Jesus said it was the one needful thing—the one thing which could never be taken away. Because of what you learn from Him and of Him, you'll always have something to hang onto—and it won't be by your fingernails!

REFLECTIONS

....

....

....

....

....

❧ 95 ❧

God's Will Alone

Every word of God is tested; He is a shield to those who take refuge in Him.

PROVERBS 30:5

Another part of waiting on the Lord is telling God that you want only what He wants—whatever that is. Does that sound terrifying? Not if you make it a practice to do the first thing: Sit at His feet and know Him.

REFLECTIONS

❧ 96 ❧

No Other Agenda

For am I now seeking the favor of men,
or of God? Or am I striving to please men?
If I were still trying to please men, I would
not be a bond-servant of Christ.

Galatians 1:10

If you will give God your reputation, if you will seek no agenda other than God's, if you are willing to do His will no matter the cost, then His life will be your life...and your life, His!

REFLECTIONS

97

Do It!

Trust in the LORD with all your heart,
and do not lean on your own understanding.
In all your ways acknowledge Him,
and He will make your paths straight.

PROVERBS 3:5,6

If you are making a habit of sitting at Jesus' feet, then whatever God says to you, do it with confidence and without hesitation.

REFLECTIONS

....

....

....

....

....

❧ 98 ❧

Set Apart unto God

...who has saved us, and called us with a holy calling, not according to our works, but according to His own purpose and grace which was granted us in Christ Jesus from all eternity.

2 TIMOTHY 1:9

Holy, means to be set apart unto God. Another word for holy is "sanctified." This means that because God has set us aside for Himself, our lives—all that we are and do—are to be set apart for Him.

REFLECTIONS

....

....

....

....

....

❧ 99 ❧

Eternal Dividends

For you have been bought with a price: therefore glorify God in your body.

1 Corinthians 6:20

Even our bodies are not our own. We cannot do with them as we want and please God. If we sow to the flesh, we will reap corruption. But if we sow to the Spirit, we will reap eternal dividends.

REFLECTIONS

....

....

....

....

....

❧ 100 ❧

Holiness Is Possible!

You shall be holy, for I am holy.

1 Peter 1:16

Precious child of God, if God says you are to be holy, then holiness is possible! Are you investing in those things which build up, nurture, and edify? Or in those things which are going to snare you, entrap you, or make you ashamed?

REFLECTIONS

....

....

....

....

....

❧ 101 ❧

Make Time for God

And it was at this time that He went off to the mountain to pray, and He spent the whole night in prayer to God.

LUKE 6:12

There are so many people naming the name of Christ who do not make time for God—time to get to know Him...time to meet with Him daily... time to pray...time to study His Word. Their time is consumed by self—then it's gone, never to be redeemed, because it hasn't been spent on eternal values. Even Jesus made time to be alone with the Father.

REFLECTIONS

....

....

....

....

....

❧ 102 ❧

Redeem the Time

Therefore be careful how you walk, not as unwise men, but as wise, making the most of your time, because the days are evil.

Ephesians 5:15,16

God commands us to redeem the time—to buy it back, to control it and not to let it control us—because the days are evil. God wants us to invest our time and energies in things that have eternal value and in people whom He created for Himself, not in things which are useless, temporal, self-centered, or destructive!

REFLECTIONS

103

What About Money?

Let your character be free from the love of money, being content with what you have; for He Himself has said, "I will never desert you, nor will I ever forsake you."

HEBREWS 13:5

Beloved, we've talked about time—what about money? What are you doing with your money? Are you spending it on earthly treasures or are you making eternal investments? Have you prayed about your resources lately? Find out how God wants you to use your time and your money. No matter what it costs, forsake all that is not of God.

REFLECTIONS

....

....

....

....

....

104

Walk Circumspectly

He has told you, O man, what is good;
and what does the LORD require of you
but to do justice, to love kindness, and to
walk humbly with your God?

MICAH 6:8

How my heart is burdened by the awful harvest so many are reaping...the pain, the destruction they've fallen into—and the futility of it all! How we need to take a good look at what we are doing with our lives, our time, our energies, our bodies. As beloved children, we must be vigilant and walk circumspectly.

REFLECTIONS

....

....

....

....

....

105

The Untold End

Therefore you too now have sorrow;
but I will see you again, and your heart will
rejoice, and no one takes your joy away from you.

John 16:22

Suspended between heaven and hell, Jesus was taunted, rejected, cursed. So much had been expected of Him. So much proclaimed. Yet there He hung—raw, beaten, bloody, gasping for breath. He looked like a loser, but the end of His story hadn't been told...and neither, Beloved, has the end of your story or mine!

REFLECTIONS

....

....

....

....

....

106

God's Message of Victory

Therefore, since Christ has suffered in the flesh, arm yourselves also with the same purpose, because he who has suffered in the flesh has ceased from sin, so as to live the rest of the time in the flesh no longer for the lusts of men, but for the will of God.

1 PETER 4:1,2

The cross takes care of the past. The cross takes care of the flesh. The cross takes care of the world with its lusts and boastful pride. The cross is God's means of victory. It is also the path of ministry.

REFLECTIONS

....

....

....

....

....

✤ 107 ✤

Winners

And Thou hast made them to be a kingdom and priests to our God; and they will reign upon the earth.

REVELATION 5:10

We belong to Jesus, and Jesus belongs to God! We have been made part of a kingdom of priests who will reign with Him when He comes to earth again as King of kings and Lord of lords. As children of God, we are winners, simply by faith in our Lord Jesus Christ!

REFLECTIONS

108

Free Indeed!

If therefore the Son shall make you free, you shall be free indeed.

John 8:36

All the world's counsel won't set you free from sin. In fact, people may call you "an addict." Sin is addictive. But Jesus came to set us free, to redeem us from the slave market of sin—and that's what He'll do for you. So give up, Beloved, and turn your life over to Him.

REFLECTIONS

....

....

....

....

....

❧ 109 ❧

The Sanctuary of God!

When I pondered to understand this, it was troublesome in my sight until I came into the sanctuary of God; then I perceived their end.

PSALM 73:16,17

In Psalm 73, the psalmist tells how envious and discouraged he was when he looked at the apparent prosperity and ease of the wicked. Bitterness crept into his life—until he went into the sanctuary of God. There is a payday, someday.

REFLECTIONS

....

....

....

....

....

❧ 110 ❧

Communing with God

When my heart was embittered...I was like a beast before Thee. Nevertheless I am continually with Thee; Thou hast taken hold of my right hand. With Thy counsel Thou wilt guide me.

Psalm 73:21-24

In the sanctuary" is an Old Testament metaphor for communing with God. The Tabernacle was a sanctuary where God dwelt among His people. God wanted them to see that all life was to be centered around communion with Him. Why? Because without His perspective, our Father knows we always end up in frustration, confusion, or destruction.

REFLECTIONS

....

....

....

....

....

❧ III ❧

A Proper Perspective

For the word of God is living and active and sharper than any two-edged sword, and piercing as far as the division of soul and spirit, of both joints and marrow, and able to judge the thoughts and intentions of the heart.

Hebrews 4:12

In the sanctuary, in our communion with God, we gain a proper perspective of life. As we thoughtfully read and meditate on the Word of God, moving through it book by book, God speaks to us. His words, His precepts become a measurement, a divine assessment for our own lives—our values, our desires, our behavior...and what we are to think and believe.

REFLECTIONS

....

....

....

....

....

112

Do You Need Strength?

Strength and beauty are in His sanctuary.

Psalm 96:6

Precious one, have you ever thought, "It would just be easier to die"? That thought entered my mind one day. But because I live in the Word, I knew it was not from God. Satan is the liar, a murderer. So I ran to the sanctuary of God's presence and there received strength to go on...strength to resist, to persist. What about you? Do you need strength?

REFLECTIONS

....

....

....

....

....

❧ 113 ❧

Discovering Beauty

O God, Thou art awesome from Thy sanctuary.
The God of Israel Himself gives strength and
power to the people. Blessed be God!

Psalm 68:35

In the sanctuary we discover beauty: the beauty of His presence, the beauty of His person, the beauty of His purpose for our life. In the sanctuary we know His imprint. Then in the world we become an expression of who He is.

REFLECTIONS

....

....

....

....

....

The Nearness of God

But as for me, the nearness of God is my good; I have made the Lord GOD *my refuge.*

PSALM 73:28

Knowing God's unlimited sovereignty and unconditional love imparts a beauty to life...and to YOU. Lines of stress, wrinkles of frustration, creases of bitterness are lifted from your face as you quietly, unhurriedly sit before your God...reading His Word, stopping to pray, sorting things out, confessing, and listening. Then you can say Psalm 73:28 with the psalmist.

REFLECTIONS

❧ 115 ❧

Answers to Our Problems

I know whom I have believed and I am convinced that He is able to guard what I have entrusted to Him until that day.

2 Timothy 1:12

As I listen to others and review my own life, I am more and more convinced that the answers to our problems are not found in "four principles of this and that" or in positive confession and positive beliefs (note that I said positive, not proper!) but in an intimate, knowledgeable relationship with our Father God and our Lord and Savior Jesus Christ.

REFLECTIONS

....

....

....

....

....

Surrounded by Skeptics?

Flesh and blood did not reveal this to you,
but My Father who is in heaven.

MATTHEW 16:17

Are you surrounded by skeptics? Dear friend, don't try to defend God! Simply explain Him as the Word of God explains Him. It's your responsibility to give them the Word. It is God's responsibility to open their eyes and turn them from darkness to light.

REFLECTIONS

....

....

....

....

....

God Is Infinite

Woe to the one who quarrels with his maker—an earthenware vessel among the vessels of earth! Will the clay say to the potter, "What are you doing?"

Isaiah 45:9

Is it hard for you when a skeptic points out man's inhumanity toward man and asks where God is? Skeptics don't understand. Our God is infinite. He sees all, knows all, and is eternal. He allows evil (Isaiah 45:7). He can intervene and many times He does, but only when it fulfills His eternal purpose.

REFLECTIONS

Jesus Is Coming

The Lord is not slow about His promise, as some count slowness, but is patient toward you, not wishing for any to perish but for all to come to repentance.

2 PETER 3:9

For so long now, so many have looked for and talked about the second coming of Jesus Christ. Generations have lived in that expectation. But He still hasn't come. Have we put our hopes on a myth? Oh, no! It's just that there are yet some to be added to His invisible church, the company of believers, the bride of Christ. Be patient, and stay alert. He'll come any day now, and you want to be ready.

REFLECTIONS

⚜ 119 ⚜

Walk On in Faith

The vision is yet for the appointed time;
it hastens toward the goal, and it will not fail....
The righteous will live by his faith.

HABAKKUK 2:3,4

The prophet Habakkuk was frustrated by the deep sin and corruption surrounding him. What was his recourse? God—and God is enough. So, Beloved, like the prophet we must lay our questions, anxieties, and impotence at the feet of God and walk on—in faith. Judgment is coming; so is Jesus.

REFLECTIONS

....

....

....

....

....

Do Not Fear!

Do not fear! Stand by and see
the salvation of the LORD.

EXODUS 14:13

I do not know your specific trial or frustration, my friend. I do not know the anxieties of your battle. But God does and you are precious to Him. What you do not understand, what you feel unable to cope with, can be overcome moment by moment if you will live by faith, taking God at His word and seeking His direction in prayer.

REFLECTIONS

Unbelief Is Sin!

In everything give thanks; for this is God's will for you in Christ Jesus.

1 THESSALONIANS 5:18

Many of us know today's Scripture backward and forward, but it's hard to believe we should give thanks when we cannot see any earthly reason for what has happened! Yet, my friend, hard or not, when we do not give thanks, we are walking in unbelief. And unbelief is sin!

REFLECTIONS

God Is in Control

The mind of man plans his way,
but the L*ORD directs his steps.*

PROVERBS 16:9

Do you ever think, "I missed it!" Maybe you did, but could it be that God had something else in mind? I must admit I was a little stressed when I missed a connecting flight in Philadelphia. If I had been in control, I wouldn't have missed the plane! *However, I would have missed what God had in mind*—a precious flight attendant who needed Jesus.

REFLECTIONS

✣ 123 ✣

Give Thanks in Everything

For as high as the heavens are above the earth, so great is His lovingkindness toward those who fear Him.

PSALM 103:11

Because our sovereign God is never out of control, because He rules over all—the small and the big things of life, the tragedies and triumphs—and because He loves us with an everlasting love—we can give thanks in everything.

REFLECTIONS

....

....

....

....

....

124

The Coming of the Lord

For you yourselves know full well that the day of the Lord will come just like a thief in the night.

1 THESSALONIANS 5:2

Suppose, just suppose, that you knew the coming of the Lord was near. Suppose you knew for certain that soon you would be standing before your God, giving an account of how you have lived as His child. Would it make a difference in the way you live today? Next month? Are you making the most of the time He's given you?

REFLECTIONS

⁂ 125 ⁂

Be Careful How You Walk

Therefore be careful how you walk,
not as unwise men, but as wise.

EPHESIANS 5:15

Did you know that we are accountable to God for all of these things? What we have been given (Matthew 25:1-30). What we know (Luke 12:4-48). Our stewardship of God's Word (1 Corinthians 4:1-5). What we teach others (James 3:1; 1 Corinthians 3:10-15). Our giving (Philippians 4:14-17). Our words (Matthew 12:36,37). And our leadership (Hebrews 13:17).

REFLECTIONS

....

....

....

....

....

"I'm Accountable"

Has the LORD as much delight in burnt offerings and sacrifices as in obeying the voice of the LORD? Behold, to obey is better than sacrifice, and to heed than the fat of rams.

1 SAMUEL 15:22

Today, would you turn back to the Scriptures listed in yesterday's thought? Look them up, one by one, mark them in your Bible in a special way, or write "I'm accountable" in the margin next to the verse. Then ask God to search your heart in each area in the light of His Word. If you'll do this, God will imprint these in your mind.

REFLECTIONS

....

....

....

....

....

127

Set Specific Goals

So teach us to number our days, that we may present to Thee a heart of wisdom.

PSALM 90:12

In the light of what you learned yesterday, why not set some specific goals for your life? For instance, because you are accountable to God for knowing His will and for doing it, you may need to plan how you are going to make the time to be alone with Him in His Word so that He can speak to you.

REFLECTIONS

Formulate Definite Plans

The Lord GOD has given me the tongue of disciples,
that I may know how to sustain the weary one with
a word. He awakens me morning by morning,
He awakens My ear to listen as a disciple.

ISAIAH 50:4

As you set your goals, formulate definite plans to reach them. For instance, to follow through on yesterday's example of making time to be with God, schedule your day to allow yourself uninterrupted time to be alone with Him. It's best to begin the day in His Word, at His feet.

REFLECTIONS

....

....

....

....

....

Take Action

For even though I am absent in body, nevertheless I am with you in spirit, rejoicing to see your good discipline and the stability of your faith in Christ.

Colossians 2:5

Once you have set goals and made your plans, begin! It's been said that it takes 21 days of repetition to form a habit. So determine that for the next 21 consecutive days you are going to take time to be alone with God and in His Word.

REFLECTIONS

Days of Cleansing

Therefore, since we have so great a cloud of witnesses surrounding us, let us also lay aside every encumbrance, and the sin which so easily entangles us, and let us run with endurance the race that is set before us.

Hebrews 12:1

Now, begin examining every other aspect of your life in the light of His coming. The days ahead will become days of cleansing as you put away those things—sins, habits, possessions, activities, and excesses that encumber you and keep you from pursuing His holiness.

REFLECTIONS

131

Eternal Dividends

Therefore, my beloved brethren,
be steadfast, immovable, always abounding
in the work of the Lord, knowing that your
toil is not in vain in the Lord.

1 CORINTHIANS 15:58

Someday Jesus will appear. It could be tomorrow or years away. Whenever, Beloved, you are to be waiting and watching, not sleeping—but occupied until He comes. Your diligence will pay eternal dividends. When Jesus comes, He'll bring your reward with Him (Revelation 22:12).

REFLECTIONS

....

....

....

....

....

My Stronghold

My soul waits in silence for God only; from Him is my salvation. He only is my rock and my salvation, my stronghold; I shall not be greatly shaken.

PSALM 62:1,2

Has God ever seemed so distant that the joy of His presence seemed lost to you? Heaven is silent. Winter has set in. Your heart shivers. It is in these times that we draw on all that we have learned from His Word, all that we know of His character and His ways, and blanket ourselves in these truths.

REFLECTIONS

....

....

....

....

....

❧ 133 ❧

God's Purpose Is Victory

Neither death, nor life, nor angels, nor principalities, nor things present, nor things to come, nor powers, nor height, nor depth, nor any other created thing, shall be able to separate us from the love of God, which is in Christ Jesus our Lord.

Romans 8:38,39

Even when we cannot hear him, God's purpose is always victory, not defeat. He has not abandoned us, the work of His hands. Oh, no! God will never separate Himself from one of His children.

REFLECTIONS

Periods of Silence

*Who is among you that fears the Lord,
that obeys the voice of His servant, that walks in
darkness and has no light? Let him trust in the
name of the Lord and rely on his God.*

ISAIAH 50:10

In any intimate relationship there are always periods of silence. God may be silent because He has spoken and we have not responded—so He waits. Or His silence may be a test of our faith. Whatever His reason, we can rely on God—even in His silence.

REFLECTIONS

⚜ 135 ⚜

Cling to God's Promises

Unto thee will I cry, O Lord my rock;
be not silent to me.

Psalm 28:1 (KJV)

When God is silent we must steep ourselves in His Word and cling to His promises. Cling, until He breaks the silence. There is always a reason for what God does—a purpose under heaven. And when He does break the silence, our relationship with Him will be more treasured than before.

REFLECTIONS

....

....

....

....

....

❧ 136 ❧

This Precious Truth

He Himself has said, "I will never desert you, nor will I ever forsake you," so that we confidently say, "The Lord is my helper, I will not be afraid."

Hebrews 13:5,6

When we walk with God in the silent times, He becomes all that matters—not our emotions, not our desires, not our pleasures. We begin to walk in meekness, accepting everything as coming from God without murmuring, disputing, or retaliating. This precious truth becomes ours.

REFLECTIONS

....

....

....

....

....

God Is There

Now to Him who is able to keep you from stumbling, and to make you stand in the presence of His glory blameless with great joy, to the only God our Savior, through Jesus Christ our Lord, be glory, majesty, dominion and authority.

JUDE 24,25

Whether we feel God's watchcare or not, whether we sense His presence or not, He is there—never ceasing to love us with His everlasting love and never failing to cause all things to work together for our good. God is never there to point to your defeat; rather, He's there to make sure you succeed.

REFLECTIONS

....

....

....

....

....

A Good Work Perfected

He who began a good work in you will perfect it until the day of Christ Jesus.

PHILIPPIANS 1:6

What God begins, God completes.

REFLECTIONS

❧ 139 ❧

In This Life We Are Expendable

But even if I am being poured out as a drink offering upon the sacrifice and service of your faith, I rejoice and share my joy with you all.

PHILIPPIANS 2:17

We human beings don't handle rejection very well. When persecution and trials come, our natural tendency is to wonder what we have done wrong to bring us into such painful difficulty. We forget—or perhaps we've never learned—that in this life we are expendable for the sake of the furtherance of the gospel.

REFLECTIONS

....

....

....

....

....

❧ 140 ❧

Never Apart from His Love

Who shall separate us from the love of Christ?

Romans 8:35

At times the Lord may seem distant, far away, unreachable. But you are never apart from His love, His promises, from Himself. Silence? It's possible. Separation? Absolutely impossible.

REFLECTIONS

....

....

....

....

....

❧ 141 ❧

A Glorious Day

For now we see in a mirror dimly, but then face to face; now I know in part, but then I shall know fully just as I also have been fully known.

1 Corinthians 13:12

What a day, what a glorious day it will be when Jesus Christ returns. Never again will there be a feeling of distance between you and your Lord. Never again shall a doubt of His love violate your faith. Hallelujah!

REFLECTIONS

....

....

....

....

....

142

There All the Time

And He shall wipe away every tear from their eyes; and there shall no longer be any death; there shall no longer be any mourning, or crying, or pain; the first things have passed away.

Revelation 21:4

Someday we shall dwell in sweet union and communion with our God and Savior forever and ever. The final silence will be broken, and we will see Him as He is...as He has been...there all the time.

REFLECTIONS

143

Digging Diligently

How blessed are those who observe His testimonies,
who seek Him with all their heart.

PSALM 119:2

Diligently digging into God's Word book by book will take the "ho hum" out of your relationship with Him. Ask God what book of the Bible you ought to study. Then start by asking questions. Who is the book about, what are its main themes, when was it written, where did the events take place, why is this book (chapter, verse) important?* You'll be awed at what you learn.

*The International Inductive Study Bible is designed for this type of study and includes instructions to help you get the most out of Scripture.

REFLECTIONS

....

....

....

....

....

144

A Multitude of Distractions

The counsel of the LORD stands forever, the plans of His heart from generation to generation.

PSALM 33:11

I know, precious one, that life in today's world offers a multitude of distractions. But don't let them rob you of intimacy with God. Don't let them rob you of the power of God in your daily life. You'll deeply regret it if you do—for you'll find yourself unprepared for life's contingencies.

REFLECTIONS

....

....

....

....

....

Make God Your Priority

My soul languishes for Thy salvation;
I wait for Thy word.

Psalm 119:81

Intimacy with God and holiness come when you make God your priority...when you get into His Word and wait on Him to speak to you...when you wait until, in the inner man, you know He is saying, "This is the way, walk in it."

REFLECTIONS

Before God in Prayer

In the morning, O Lord, Thou wilt hear my voice; in the morning I will order my prayer to Thee and eagerly watch.

Psalm 5:3

Where do you gain great confidence in God and in His will for you each day of your life? In waiting before Him in prayer. Because your goal is not simply to know God's Word, but to know the God of the Word and roll every care, every concern, every question, every need onto His shoulders.

REFLECTIONS

....

....

....

....

....

❧ 147 ❧

Searching for the Heart of God

And you will seek Me and find Me,
when you search for Me with all your heart.
And I will be found by you.

Jeremiah 29:13,14

Don't you want to know your God so intimately that your heart touches His—that your hearts beat as one? Prayer is searching for the heart of God to know and do His will, to sense and share His love, to hear and intercede for others.

REFLECTIONS

....

....

....

....

....

148

Be Still

And after the earthquake a fire; but the LORD was not in the fire: and after the fire a still small voice.

1 KINGS 19:12 (KJV)

We must learn to do more than pray, "Bless me…give me…help me." We must meditate on His Word, be quiet before Him—still enough to hear His voice…and obey.

REFLECTIONS

....

....

....

....

....

❧ 149 ❧

Seek to Be Holy

How can a young man keep his way pure?
By keeping it according to Thy word. With all
my heart I have sought Thee; do not let me
wander from Thy commandments.

Psalm 119:9,10

God is looking for men, women, teens, and children who will tremble at His Word—for those who will respect Him as God and treat Him accordingly. Those who will believe Him...obey Him...honor Him as God...worship Him in accordance with all that He is. Will you be that person, Beloved?

REFLECTIONS

....

....

....

....

....

✤ 150 ✤

Embrace God's Cross

Always carrying about in the body the dying of Jesus, that the life of Jesus also may be manifested in our body.

2 Corinthians 4:10

Does joy seem a stranger to you? Maybe it's because you haven't embraced God's cross in your life. The words of Josif Trif, a 66-year-old Romanian pastor, explain it so clearly, "If it weren't for Communism, I would not have loved our Lord as much. I kissed the cross the Communists gave me."

REFLECTIONS

....

....

....

....

....

Kiss Your Cross

And he who does not take his cross and follow after Me is not worthy of Me.

MATTHEW 10:38

O Beloved, if you are lacking peace or joy, it might be because you are failing to walk in the sweetness of faith's obedience. Kiss your cross—it's from His sovereign hand. There's a purpose in it all...your Christlikeness.

REFLECTIONS

❧ 152 ❧

Satan's Five Deadly Ds

Your adversary, the devil, prowls about like a roaring lion, seeking someone to devour.

1 PETER 5:8

Has disappointment ever caused you to go into an emotional tailspin? Have you ever felt you might drown in discouragement? Then, my friend, you have engaged in warfare with the evil one and allowed him to penetrate your line of defense. Let's take a look at how you can be more than a conqueror over Satan's Five Deadly Ds: disappointment, discouragement, dejection, despair, and demoralization.

REFLECTIONS

....

....

....

....

....

The First Deadly D

But as for me, I trust in Thee, O Lord, I say, "Thou art my God." My times are in Thy hand.

Psalm 31:14,15

The first deadly D is Disappointment. To counterattack disappointment you need to launch the Christian's Strategic Defense System—faith that in meekness praises God in every situation by seeing it as God's sovereign appointment.

REFLECTIONS

The Second Deadly D

Have I not commanded you? Be strong and courageous! Do not tremble or be dismayed, for the LORD your God is with you wherever you go.

JOSHUA 1:9

The second deadly D is Discouragement. After Moses died, God was careful to admonish Joshua to "be strong and courageous." Years earlier the Israelites believed the report of the spies who became discouraged by the giants in the land God had given them to occupy. So they wandered in the wilderness for 40 years! What about you? Have you listened to the world's analysis of your condition rather than courageously believing your God?

REFLECTIONS

155

The Third Deadly D

But as for me, I will hope continually, and will praise Thee yet more and more.

Psalm 71:14

Have you ever found yourself mired in the mud of Dejection? Instead of the joy of the Lord being your strength (Nehemiah 8:10), you are about to faint (Isaiah 61:3). When dejection pulls you down into its depths, reach up and take hold of His hand with the act of praise.

REFLECTIONS

....

....

....

....

....

The Fourth Deadly D

Why are you in despair, O my soul?
And why have you become disturbed within me?
Hope in God, for I shall again praise
Him for the help of His presence.

Psalm 42:5

The fourth deadly D is Despair—to despair is to lose or abandon hope. Despair leaves you apathetic, your mind is numb. O precious child of God, when you are in despair, look for a specific promise of God to counter each cause of despair. Then you will find yourself saying Psalm 42:5 with the psalmist.

REFLECTIONS

157

The Final Deadly D

For God hath not given us the spirit of fear; but of power, and of love, and of a sound mind.

2 Timothy 1:7 (KJV)

The final deadly D is Demoralization. Demoralized people run in circles—if they have the strength to run! They cannot get their act together in any of the disciplines of life. Many times they are simply paralyzed with fear. But God has not given you a spirit of fear, rather a sound mind—a mind under control. God loves you. If you are His child, you have His power. Use it.

REFLECTIONS

158

Happiness and Joy?

But even if I am being poured out as a drink offering upon the sacrifice and service of your faith, I rejoice and share my joy with you all.

Philippians 2:17

We are living in a time of unprecedented selfishness. Today the rallying cry is "Be number one." But when being number one is our goal, then everyone else must be in second place—including God. Is this what happiness and joy are all about?

REFLECTIONS

159

A Servant Mind

Have this attitude in yourselves
[or, "let this mind be in you"] *which was*
also in Christ Jesus, who, although He existed
in the form of God, did not regard equality with
God a thing to be grasped, but emptied Himself,
taking the form of a bond-servant.

PHILIPPIANS 2:5-7

The mind of Christ is a servant mind.

REFLECTIONS

Are You Willing?

But I thought it necessary to send to you Epaphroditus, my brother and fellow worker and fellow soldier, who is also your messenger and minister to my need; because he was longing for you all and was distressed because you had heard that he was sick.

PHILIPPIANS 2:25,26

Are you concerned for the spiritual welfare of others? Are you willing to give yourself to listening to them, to helping them, to meeting their needs, to showing them what God has to say in His Word? Oh, how we need to say, "Here am I, Lord. Use me. Send me."

REFLECTIONS

....

....

....

....

....

Don't Lose Heart

Fixing our eyes on Jesus, the author and perfecter of faith, who for the joy set before Him endured the cross, despising the shame, and has sat down at the right hand of the throne of God. For consider Him who has endured such hostility by sinners against Himself, so that you may not grow weary and lose heart.

HEBREWS 12:2,3

Sometimes the joy of obedience does not bring immediate results. It is then we must be reminded of the much greater burden our Lord bore in humbling Himself unto death.

REFLECTIONS

162

Losing Your Joy

For even the Son of Man did not come to be served, but to serve, and to give His life a ransom for many.

Mark 10:45

It is not people who rob us of our joy; it is our failure to have the mind of Christ. When you start to lose your joy because of people, stop and ask God, "How would You have me serve You in this situation—right now?"

REFLECTIONS

....

....

....

....

....

163

God Is Faithful

God is faithful, who will not allow you to be tempted beyond what you are able, but with the temptation will provide the way of escape also, that you may be able to endure it.

1 Corinthians 10:13

Today's Scripture, Beloved, is your assurance that God will never permit anything to come your way that you cannot handle. Whatever the trial, testing, or temptation, you can know that if it were not possible for you to endure it in a way pleasing to your heavenly Father, He would not permit it.

REFLECTIONS

....

....

....

....

....

God Does Not Tempt Us

Let no one say when he is tempted, "I am being tempted by God"; for God cannot be tempted by evil, and He Himself does not tempt anyone.

JAMES 1:13

If we think the source, the hotbed, of temptation is God, we're deceived. God is altogether holy and would not tempt us to do evil!

REFLECTIONS

....

....

....

....

....

❧ 165 ❧

The Source of Temptation

But each one is tempted when he is carried away and enticed by his own lust.

James 1:14

God wants you to realize that temptation does not come from without, but from within. Oh, the opportunity to sin is always there; however, it is not the world or the devil that causes you to be tempted—it is your own flesh!

REFLECTIONS

....

....

....

....

....

166

Child of Desire

He who is steadfast in righteousness will attain to life, and he who pursues evil will bring about his own death.

Proverbs 11:19

Sin is a child of desire. Recognize your desires for what they are. If you rationalize them and accommodate them, you will find yourself right in the middle of sin.

REFLECTIONS

❧ 167 ❧

Walk in the Spirit

But I say, walk by the Spirit, and you will not carry out the desire of the flesh.

Galatians 5:16

God does not say that our flesh will not have desires. Rather, He says that the flesh and the Spirit "are in opposition to one another" (Galatians 5:17), and because of this tension, you cannot just do as you please. You must consciously choose to walk in the Spirit.

REFLECTIONS

168

The Cravings of the Flesh

What is the source of quarrels and conflicts among you? Is not the source your pleasures that wage war in your members?

James 4:1

Don't make the mistake of thinking of desires as "needs." God promises to supply all your needs (Philippians 4:19). Needs are never contrary to His Word, but desires are the cravings of your flesh.

REFLECTIONS

....

....

....

....

....

❧ 169 ❧

Flee from Lust

Now flee from youthful lusts, and pursue righteousness, faith, love and peace, with those who call on the Lord from a pure heart.

2 TIMOTHY 2:22

You are never above temptation because it is your own lust—your own flesh—which entices you, and you will have to live with that flesh until you see the Lord. Flee from lust. In the power of the Spirit get out of there fast and get far away.

REFLECTIONS

Your On-Call Comforter

And He will give you another Helper [Comforter], that He may be with you forever.

John 14:16

Are you in a battle? Does a "Goliath" loom before you? Look up! Look up to the heavens, up to your Father's throne, up to your High Priest standing at the right hand of the Father on your behalf. Then look within! Is the Spirit of the living God not dwelling within? Is He not your resident Helper, your on-call Comforter?

REFLECTIONS

....

....

....

....

....

Divinely Powerful Weapons

The weapons of our warfare are not of the flesh, but divinely powerful for the destruction of fortresses.

2 Corinthians 10:4

Stop and think about the story of David and Goliath. The Israelites facing Goliath had the same God on their side that David had on his. What made the difference? They trusted in "the arm of flesh"—thus they were defeated! *David trusted in what he knew about God.* Who are you trusting?

REFLECTIONS

....

....

....

....

....

The Lord of Hosts

You come to me with a sword, a spear, and a javelin, but I come to you in the name of the LORD *of hosts.*

1 SAMUEL 17:45

When David faced Goliath, he remembered that God was *Jehovah-sabaoth,* the Lord of hosts, which means He is the Captain of all—all principalities, powers, and spiritual forces in high places. Why do we fear Satan when we're on God's side?

REFLECTIONS

173

Proving Your Faith

Therefore, strengthen the hands that are weak and the knees that are feeble.

HEBREWS 12:12

O Beloved, don't you see? God in His sovereignty permits "Goliaths" in your life as tests...tests which give you an opportunity to prove your faith. And in proving your faith, you prove Him and, thus, are strengthened.

REFLECTIONS

No Way Out

I know, O my God, that Thou triest the heart and delightest in uprightness.

1 Chronicles 29:17

You'll never be the Christian you can be without "Goliaths." You'll never know God intimately apart from them. It's the trials, the conflicts, the adversities, the "no way out" situations, the impossibilities that drive us to God, where we discover who He is and what He is.

REFLECTIONS

❧ 175 ❧

Run "into His Name"

The name of the Lord *is a strong tower;*
the righteous runs into it and is safe.

Proverbs 18:10

I pray that you'll get to know your God by name and that in the day of adversity you'll not hesitate to call upon the name of the Lord, that you'll not hesitate to run "into His name" and be secure.

REFLECTIONS

Consider It All Joy

Consider it all joy, my brethren, when you encounter various trials, knowing that the testing of your faith produces endurance.

JAMES 1:2,3

We seem to associate only blessings with the goodness of God. How earthbound we are! How temporal our perspective! To the child of God, even trials are cause for rejoicing!

REFLECTIONS

❧ 177 ❧

"Follow Me!"

Jesus said to him, "If I want him to remain until I come, what is that to you? You follow Me!"

John 21:22

Have you ever looked at another Christian and thought, "They've got it made! They're so blessed of God!" After Jesus told Peter how he was going to suffer and die, He said to him, "Follow Me!"(John 21:19). Peter, seeing his fellow disciple John, asked Jesus what was going to happen to him. Do you know what Jesus replied?

REFLECTIONS

....

....

....

....

....

You Are Uniquely You

...that the proof of your faith, being more precious than gold which is perishable, even though tested by fire, may be found to result in praise and glory and honor at the revelation of Jesus Christ.

1 PETER 1:7

Beloved, you are not the same as any other person! You are uniquely you. So God has a unique, individual set of circumstances which He will use to refine and purify you so that you will come through the fire of affliction with the dross of your ungodliness consumed.

REFLECTIONS

❧ 179 ❧

Blessings in Disguise

In this you greatly rejoice, even though now for a little while, if necessary, you have been distressed by various trials.

1 PETER 1:6

To consider it all joy is to look down the long road to the eternal...to look beyond the trial to the end result, which is you, perfect and complete, lacking nothing. Trials are blessings in disguise.

REFLECTIONS

....

....

....

....

....

Nothing Is Hidden

For it is time for judgment to begin
with the household of God; and if it begins
with us first, what will be the outcome for those
who do not obey the gospel of God?

1 PETER 4:17

Nothing is hidden from God. We cannot pretend to be righteous on the outside while inside we are filled with unrighteousness. We can be sure our sin will find us out. The justice of God, the righteousness of God, the very character of God requires it—and will see to it!

REFLECTIONS

God's Grace Is Sufficient

And He has said to me, "My grace is sufficient for you, for power is perfected in weakness." Most gladly, therefore, I will rather boast about my weaknesses, that the power of Christ may dwell in me. Therefore I am well content with weaknesses, with insults, with distresses, with persecutions, with difficulties, for Christ's sake; for when I am weak, then I am strong.

2 CORINTHIANS 12:9,10

God's grace is not only available, it is sufficient.

REFLECTIONS

How Much Do You Hate Evil?

You have wearied the LORD with your words. Yet you say, "How have we wearied Him?"

MALACHI 2:17

How much do you hate evil? Some Christians think themselves magnanimous when they say, "There is a little bit of good in everyone, and we need to see the good. After all, God does!" Does He? Listen to how we weary God: Malachi goes on to say, "In that you say 'Everyone who does evil is good in the sight of the Lord, and He delights in them.'" We weary God when we don't agree with Him regarding evil. When we excuse sin that God must deal with. We weary God because when we do things like this we diminish His holiness.

REFLECTIONS

....

....

....

183

Your Only Allegiance

Should you help the wicked and love those who hate the LORD and so bring wrath on yourself from the LORD?

2 CHRONICLES 19:2

Doesn't today's Scripture pose an interesting question? How would you answer it, Beloved? What is your alliance with the ungodly? What is your allegiance to them? Your only allegiance ought to be the love of God that would mourn over their sin and seek to rescue them from judgment.

REFLECTIONS

....

....

....

....

....

❧ 184 ❧

God Never Compromises

Wash yourselves, make yourselves clean; remove the evil of your deeds from My sight. Cease to do evil, learn to do good; seek justice, reprove the ruthless; defend the orphan, plead for the widow.

Isaiah 1:16,17

Compromising men and women may call evil good in the sight of the Lord and say that God delights in them, but that is a lie. God never compromises with evil; He only exposes evil for what it is and then judges it. Remember, Beloved, you serve a holy God.

REFLECTIONS

....

....

....

....

....

185

Pray for Our Land Today!

First of all, then, I urge that entreaties and prayers, petitions and thanksgivings, be made on behalf of all men, for kings and all who are in authority, in order that we may lead a tranquil and quiet life in all godliness and dignity.

1 Timothy 2:1,2

Pray for our land today!
Intercede for our leaders.

Pray that men and women will turn from their wickedness and bow in godly repentance.

Plead for God's mercy.

REFLECTIONS

....

....

....

....

....

186

Someone to Intercede

And I searched for a man among them who should build up the wall and stand in the gap before Me for the land, that I should not destroy it; but I found no one.

Ezekiel 22:30

Has it ever occurred to you that God could use your earnest prayers to change the course of our nation's history? Israel's cup of iniquity was full. Over and over God had called His people to repentance, but they would not listen. Can you hear the anguish in His voice as He looks for someone to intercede?

REFLECTIONS

....

....

....

....

....

187

Clothe Yourself in God's Armor

No man has authority to restrain the wind with the wind, or authority over the day of death; and there is no discharge in the time of war, and evil will not deliver those who practice it.

Ecclesiastes 8:8

If we diligently intercede for our nation, perhaps God will stay His hand of judgment and bring revival. Beloved, now is not the time to be sleeping. Now is the time to use our weapons of warfare. Clothe yourself in His armor, take up the weapons He has given you, and fight the good fight of faith.

REFLECTIONS

Pray Diligently

"Woe is me, for I am ruined! Because I am a man of unclean lips, and I live among a people of unclean lips..." Then one of the seraphim flew to me, with a burning coal in his hand which he had taken from the altar with tongs. And he touched my mouth with it and said, "Behold, this has touched your lips; and your iniquity is taken away, and your sin is forgiven."

Isaiah 6:5-7

As you begin to pray diligently, God will use your intercession to make you more like the man or woman of God you long to be. You can't be in His presence praying earnestly and not be changed!

REFLECTIONS

....

....

....

....

....

❧ 189 ❧

Cast Your Care on God

Surely I have composed and quieted my soul; like a weaned child rests against his mother.

Psalm 131:2

It's hard to trust God when the "forecast" is contrary to what we feel we need, isn't it? Maybe it's a restored relationship, and the forecast is grim. Maybe it's a job, and the outlook is bleak. What do you do? What can you do? You can cast all your care on the One who cares for you.

REFLECTIONS

....

....

....

....

....

God's Mighty Hand

Thou hast a strong arm; Thy hand is mighty,
Thy right hand is exalted.

Psalm 89:13

God has you in His hand, and His hand is a mighty hand. Mighty not only to save and to keep, but mighty to deliver. He brought the children of Israel "out of Egypt with a mighty hand, when they cried to Him" (Deuteronomy 9:26; Exodus 2:23-25). Can He not also deliver you with His mighty hand?

REFLECTIONS

....

....

....

....

....

191

The Lord Is My Helper

Let your character be free from the love of money, being content with what you have; for He Himself has said, "I will never desert you, nor will I ever forsake you," so that we confidently say, "The Lord *is my helper, I will not be afraid. What shall man do to me?"*

Hebrews 13:5,6

Has God not promised to "supply all your needs according to His riches in glory in Christ Jesus" (Philippians 4:19)? God is immutable; He cannot change. He cannot lie. He will not leave you nor forsake you.

REFLECTIONS

192

God Cares for You

Humble yourselves, therefore, under the mighty hand of God, that He may exalt you at the proper time, casting all your anxiety upon Him, because He cares for you.

1 PETER 5:6,7

Beloved, roll that burden, that care, that anxiety, that weight off your back and onto God's almighty shoulders. You are the sheep of His pasture, and sheep are not burden-bearing animals! He cares for you. He cares for you. (Have you got that? He cares for you!)

REFLECTIONS

....

....

....

....

....

193

Cry to God

Who among all these does not know that the hand of the LORD has done this, in whose hand is the life of every living thing, and the breath of all mankind?

Job 12:9,10

He is God! Cry to Him. If it is for your good and His glory, God will answer your cry. If not, He won't, because what He has planned is better. The plans God has for you are plans for good and not for evil, to give you a future and a hope (Jeremiah 29:11).

REFLECTIONS

God Hates Divorce

"I hate divorce," says the LORD, the God of Israel.

MALACHI 2:16

Has there ever been a time, even for one second, when you have thought it might be nice to be divorced? How I appreciate those who, though living with mates who are talking about divorce, desire to know what God says about it in His Word and act accordingly. Our marriages and commitment to one another are to be earthly pictures of Jesus Christ's unconditional, sacrificial love for His bride, the church.

REFLECTIONS

195

Marriage Is a Covenant

Husbands, love your wives, just as Christ also loved the church and gave Himself up for her.

Ephesians 5:25

Do you know why God hates divorce? First, because marriage is a covenant, and covenants are not to be broken. God made a covenant with Israel. He also made a covenant with the church, the new covenant in Jesus' blood, which grants us grace that leads to eternal life. He'll never break that covenant.

REFLECTIONS

....

....

....

....

....

Divorce Distorts

For this cause a man shall leave his father and mother, and shall cleave to his wife; and the two shall become one flesh. This mystery is great; but I am speaking with reference to Christ and the church.

EPHESIANS 5:31,32

The second reason God hates divorce is that marriage is a picture of our covenant union with the Lord Jesus Christ. Earthly marriages are to be a picture of our heavenly marriage to Him. God hates divorce because it distorts the picture of His eternal commitment to us.

REFLECTIONS

....

....

....

....

....

❧ 197 ❧

God Will Justify the Innocent

We shall know by this that we are of the truth, and shall assure our heart before Him, in whatever our heart condemns us; for God is greater than our heart, and knows all things.

1 John 3:19,20

I know there are many of you who never desired a divorce and who now feel like a second-class citizen in the family of God. Don't heap upon yourself a condemnation that is not from God. Someday those things that are hidden now will be revealed for what they are. God will justify the innocent and clear those unjustly declared guilty by man.

REFLECTIONS

....

....

....

....

....

❧ 198 ❧

Answered Prayers

I planted, Apollos watered,
but God was causing the growth.

1 Corinthians 3:6

We don't always know how our prayers will be answered, do we? I cannot tell you how often I have shared the gospel with someone sitting next to me on a plane and thought: "Their grandparents, mother, father, or wife would be so excited if only they knew how their prayers are being answered right now!"

REFLECTIONS

....

....

....

....

....

❧ 199 ❧

God Is at Work

How then shall they call upon Him in whom they have not believed? And how shall they believe in Him whom they have not heard? And how shall they hear without a preacher?

Romans 10:14

You may not see it—but God is at work. He has a Father's heart; the world is on His heart. But He needs men and women who are established in His Word and not ashamed to share the gospel of Jesus Christ—it is the power of God unto salvation to everyone who believes, both Jew and Gentile.

REFLECTIONS

....

....

....

....

....

200

Our Time Is Short

For who is our hope or joy or crown of exultation? Is it not even you, in the presence of our Lord Jesus at His coming? For you are our glory and joy.

1 THESSALONIANS 2:19,20

Our time is short—shorter than we think. And we can't take anything with us when this life is over—except the souls we have invested in.

REFLECTIONS

Handling Disappointment

He knows the way I take; when He has tried me, I shall come forth as gold.

Job 23:10

How do you handle disappointment so that you don't walk away from life thinking, "Well, it's all over now. I'll never be the same. I'll never have what I've wanted. It's gone...forever"? You handle it, my friend, by understanding that *disappointment is God's appointment.*

REFLECTIONS

Disappointment: A Trial of Faith

Behold, like the clay in the potter's hand, so are you in My hand.

JEREMIAH 18:6

Disappointment is a trial of your faith. Disappointment is something which, strange as it may seem, has been filtered through God's sovereign fingers of love. He has allowed disappointment to slip through His fingers into your life, which He holds in the palm of His omnipotent hand. It has a purpose. It's for the shaping of you into a beautiful vessel of praise, honor, and glory at His coming.

REFLECTIONS

....

....

....

....

....

❧ 203 ❧

Testing Your Faith

The testing of your faith produces endurance. And let endurance have its perfect result, that you may be perfect and complete, lacking in nothing.

James 1:3,4

Why should you consider it all joy when you encounter various trials—when you are overwhelmed with pain, captured by disappointment? Because your God commands it. And He commands it because your obedient response will be the making of you, the strengthening of your faith.

REFLECTIONS

Exult in Your Tribulations

We also exult in our tribulations, knowing that tribulation brings about perseverance; and perseverance, proven character....

ROMANS 5:3,4

If the disappointment, the trial, were not for your benefit and His glory, God would never have permitted it. He wants you to have every opportunity to be Christlike and fruitful. God doesn't want you to have any regrets when you see Him face-to-face.

REFLECTIONS

....

....

....

....

....

❧ 205 ❧

His Perfect Will

The steps of a man are established by the LORD;
and He delights in his way.

PSALM 37:23

It took more than 20 years before God revealed what He had in mind when He took Jack and me off the mission field. In my disappointment, I simply had to come to the point where I would obey His command and count it all joy—knowing He would use it to make me more like Christ and to accomplish His perfect will. (Now Precept is in more than 110 countries and 38 languages—and I stand in awe!)

REFLECTIONS

....

....

....

....

....

206

Enduring Heartache

The Lord is near to the brokenhearted,
and saves those who are crushed in spirit.

Psalm 34:18

Christians are not exempt from heartache, but we do have the means to endure heartache without falling apart. For this we have Jesus...His grace, His sufficiency. For this we have His Word... His promises, His wisdom.

REFLECTIONS

❧ 207 ❧

The Cure for Heartache

Heal me, O Lord, and I will be healed; save me and I will be saved, for Thou art my praise.

Jeremiah 17:14

I cannot change others' circumstances; I cannot cure their heartache. I cannot change my own circumstances or cure my own heartache! But I know who can. The cure for heartache is found in the Great Physician, Jehovah-rapha, and His healing balm of Gilead, the Word of God.

REFLECTIONS

208

Teach People the Word

Jesus therefore answered them, and said, "My teaching is not Mine, but His who sent Me."

John 7:16

Teaching people the Word, showing them where to turn in the midst of their pain and confusion, helping them develop and deepen their relationship with Jesus Christ—that is what will make the difference in their difficult circumstances.

REFLECTIONS

....

....

....

....

....

Comforting Others

Blessed be the God and Father of our Lord Jesus Christ, the Father of mercies and God of all comfort; who comforts us in all our affliction so that we may be able to comfort those who are in any affliction with the comfort with which we ourselves are comforted by God.

2 CORINTHIANS 1:3,4

Our God comforts us so that we may be able, with that comfort...that grace...that strength, to comfort others. Don't waste your sorrows—help someone else.

REFLECTIONS

❧ 210 ❧

An Eternal Weight of Glory

For momentary, light affliction
is producing for us an eternal weight of
glory far beyond all comparison.

2 Corinthians 4:17

Your heartaches and hurts are the very tools God will use to transform you into the image of His Son.

REFLECTIONS

....

....

....

....

....

211

An Ambassador for Christ

I have fought the good fight, I have finished the course, I have kept the faith; in the future there is laid up for me the crown of righteousness, which the Lord, the righteous Judge, will award to me on that day; and not only to me, but also to all who have loved His appearing.

2 Timothy 4:7,8

You are an ambassador for Christ, pointing others away from things which are seen (the temporal) to things which are not seen (the eternal). So take courage, valiant warrior. Fight the good fight of faith, for soon it will be over and you'll be on the Victor's side, with the King you represented.

REFLECTIONS

212

Bear Fruit

Truly, truly, I say to you, unless a grain of wheat falls into the earth and dies, it remains by itself alone; but if it dies, it bears much fruit.

John 12:24

A crucified life cannot help but change things... and people.

REFLECTIONS

....

....

....

....

....

A Shining Light

Let your light shine before men in such a way that they may see your good works, and glorify your Father who is in heaven.

Matthew 5:16

The world is looking for people who really live according to what they say they believe. What—whom—do they see in you?

REFLECTIONS

....

....

....

....

....

❧ 214 ❧

God Is Able!

LORD, who is like Thee?

PSALM 35:10

Today wouldn't it be good to remember that God is able to change the hearts and minds of men and women...able and willing to supply all of our needs...able to move heaven and earth...able to cause all things to work together for our good and His glory? He is able!

REFLECTIONS

....

....

....

....

....

A Way of Life

Jesus therefore answered and was saying to them, "Truly, truly, I say to you, the Son can do nothing of Himself, unless it is something He sees the Father doing; for whatever the Father does, these things the Son also does in like manner."

John 5:19

Prayer is to be a way of life: a constant communion that causes you to commit everything to your Father for His leadership, His anointing, His provision according to His way and according to His time. Live as Jesus lived.

REFLECTIONS

216

Effective Prayer

If you abide in Me, and My words abide in you, ask whatever you wish, and it shall be done for you.

John 15:7

Effective prayer, that which is born of the Spirit, does not rip verses out of context and fling them at the feet of God's footstool, demanding that God come through. Effective prayer comes when we abide in Him and His words abide in us, and we ask according to His will.

REFLECTIONS

....

....

....

....

....

He Is Waiting

Then the LORD God called to the man,
and said to him, "Where are you?"

GENESIS 3:9

Adam and Eve had just sinned. They had eaten of the forbidden fruit and were hiding from God. Yet God, who is omnipresent and omniscient, asked them where they were. God knew, but did they? Pause and take a good look at where you are, and why you're there. If you think you can hide something from God, you're wrong. Confess it. Get out in the open with God and walk with Him again in faith's obedience.

REFLECTIONS

218

The Lord Hears

The righteous cry and the LORD hears, and delivers them out of all their troubles.

PSALM 34:17

I have been reading through the Old Testament for my quiet time, and I don't think I have ever been as aware as I am now of how sensitive God is to the cries of His people. How often I have reminded our Father of that lately as I have cried out to Him in my impotence. And He has not failed me. Why? Because He is the unchangeable, faithful Father who keeps His Word.

REFLECTIONS

....

....

....

....

....

Dependent upon God

Then Isaiah...sent to Hezekiah saying, "Thus says the LORD, the God of Israel, 'Because you have prayed to Me about Sennacherib king of Assyria, I have heard you.'"

2 KINGS 19:20

O Beloved, what would happen if we prayed more? God's ears are never closed to the cries of His creation. When we consult God—seeking His will, His guidance, His assistance—we are humbling ourselves. We're saying, "God, I am dependent upon you."

REFLECTIONS

To Him Be the Glory

For who has known the mind of the Lord, or who became His counselor? Or who has first given to Him that it might be paid back to him again? For from Him and through Him and to Him are all things. To Him be the glory forever. Amen.

Romans 11:34-36

When we don't pray—or when our prayers really amount to telling God what to do—we make ourselves wiser than God by telling Him how to direct the affairs of a universe that He brought into existence and sustains without any help from us. We walk in pride, saying, "I can handle life myself."

REFLECTIONS

221

A Friend of the World

You adulteresses, do you not know that friendship with the world is hostility toward God? Therefore whoever wishes to be a friend of the world makes himself an enemy of God.

James 4:4

Christianity never removes us from the evil world...it leaves us in it. But we are not to be of that world. We are not to think like the world, adapt to the world, or sell out to the world. Instead, we are to contest the world, oppose it, refuse to be conformed to it.

REFLECTIONS

....

....

....

....

....

❧ 222 ❧

Know the Truth

And have mercy on some, who are doubting; save others, snatching them out of the fire; and on some have mercy with fear, hating even the garment polluted by the flesh.

JUDE 22,23

Jesus never called us to peaceful coexistence and compromise with the world and its temporary prince. Jesus leaves us here to rescue the hearts and minds of men and women and children so that they might know the truth.

REFLECTIONS

❧ 223 ❧

Faithful Until Death

Be faithful until death, and I will give you the crown of life.

Revelation 2:10

Where are the people who are willing to seek the truth no matter what the cost? Who are willing to risk their career, their safety, their security, their all for the truth embodied in our Lord Jesus Christ? Are you one such person, Beloved? A crown awaits!

REFLECTIONS

....

....

....

....

....

The Light of God's Word

*As a result, we are no longer to be children...
carried about by every wind of doctrine,
by the trickery of men...but speaking the
truth in love, we are to grow up in all aspects
into Him, who is the head, even Christ.*

Ephesians 4:14,15

God's Word must be propagated; it must be shared and taught. Others need to learn how to study His Word for themselves so that they won't be carried about by every wind of doctrine and cunning craftiness of this evil world. They need to know it so that they, like you, can live in the light of it.

REFLECTIONS

Are You Being Threatened?

Then this Daniel began distinguishing himself among the commissioners and satraps because he possessed an extraordinary spirit....Then the commissioners and satraps began trying to find a ground of accusation against Daniel....But they could find no ground of accusation or evidence of corruption, inasmuch as he was faithful, and no negligence or corruption was to be found in him.

DANIEL 6:3,4

Are you being threatened with loss? Loss of a loved one, loss of reputation, loss of a dream, if you remain steadfast in your pursuit of the Lord and His holiness? Be a Daniel.

REFLECTIONS

A Steadfast Relationship with God

[Daniel] continued kneeling on his knees three times a day, praying and giving thanks before his God, as he had been doing previously.

Daniel 6:10

There were no starts, no stops, no interruptions in Daniel's walk. Isn't that something? Circumstances could not alter his relationship with God. And if the powers that be didn't like it, they would just have to feed him to the lions! He'd rather die than compromise his God. How about you?

REFLECTIONS

....

....

....

....

....

Facing the Lions

Then the king gave orders, and Daniel was brought in and cast into the lions' den. The king spoke and said to Daniel, "Your God whom you constantly serve will Himself deliver you."

Daniel 6:16

When we face the lions we can know that, like Daniel, we may be tossed into their den. But we can also know that they won't devour us. Ultimately victory will come to those who constantly serve God, to those who won't lay aside their communion with Him, who won't take their eyes off Him.

REFLECTIONS

Victory Through Prayer

"Daniel, servant of the living God,
has your God, whom you constantly serve,
been able to deliver you from the lions?" Then
Daniel spoke to the king, "O king, live forever!
My God sent His angel and shut the lions' mouths,
and they have not harmed me, inasmuch as I was
found innocent before Him; and also toward you,
O king, I have committed no crime."

Daniel 6:20-22

Jealous men sought Daniel's demise, but Daniel came out the victor. Do victories like that just happen? No! They are won where Daniel's was—on our knees, in our closets, clinging to all that we know of our God.

REFLECTIONS

....

....

....

....

....

God's Dominion

I make a decree that in all the dominion of my kingdom men are to fear and tremble before the God of Daniel; for He is the living God and enduring forever, and His kingdom is one which will not be destroyed, and His dominion will be forever.

Daniel 6:26

Daniel was a man of commitment, conviction, courage, and consistency. His enemies knew it. The king knew it. His God knew it. In the end, God through Daniel brought the king to such deep conviction that King Darius issued the above decree. O that men and women would declare such things about God as a result of observing God at work in our lives.

REFLECTIONS

....

....

....

....

Your God Is a Lion Tamer!

Therefore, my beloved brethren,
be steadfast, immovable, always abounding
in the work of the Lord, knowing that your
toil is not in vain in the Lord.

1 CORINTHIANS 15:58

When your faith is challenged, when you feel threatened, remember that "by faith" Daniel "shut the mouths of lions," and you can too (Hebrews 11:33). Your God is a lion tamer!

REFLECTIONS

....

....

....

....

....

Our Struggle

Our struggle is not against flesh and blood, but against the rulers, against the powers, against the world forces of this darkness, against the spiritual forces of wickedness in the heavenly places.

EPHESIANS 6:12

Are there times when you feel as if an army has come against you? You don't know what's going to happen, but you feel it's not going to be good. What do you do? First, remember the above mentioned verse.

REFLECTIONS

The Fear You Feel

In addition to all, taking up the shield of faith with which you will be able to extinguish all the flaming missiles of the evil one....

Ephesians 6:16

There's someone behind the fear you feel—the enemy, that serpent of old, the devil, the accuser of the brethren, the father of lies. What you're imagining may or may not be fact, but either way it's torment! Satan's fiery darts have started fires that are hard to extinguish. But there's hope: taking up the shield of faith...

REFLECTIONS

233

The Battle Is the Lord's!

The captain of the LORD'S host said to Joshua, "Remove your sandals from your feet, for the place where you are standing is holy." And Joshua did so.

JOSHUA 5:15

The battle is not yours but the Lord's! And because it is His and not yours, it must be fought His way. You are to stand firm in the Lord and in the strength of His might. Deliverance comes from the Lord! Don't go into battle without the Captain of the Host.

REFLECTIONS

....

....

....

....

....

Seek the Lord

And Jehoshaphat was afraid and turned his attention to seek the Lord; *and proclaimed a fast throughout all Judah.*

2 Chronicles 20:3

Beloved, when you fear for your welfare…or when you shudder at the thought of what the future may hold…or when you simply hurt because others have come against you, you must do what Jehoshaphat, the king of Judah, did when he heard that a great multitude was coming against him.

REFLECTIONS

....

....

....

....

....

Trust God

Put your trust in the LORD your God, and you will be established. Put your trust in His prophets [in the Word] and succeed.

2 CHRONICLES 20:20

Though King Jehoshaphat was afraid and didn't know what specific action to take against the coming army, he knew where to look. And it's the same place you, Beloved, can look today.

REFLECTIONS

Ruler Over All

O LORD, the God of our fathers,
art Thou not God in the heavens? And art
Thou not ruler over all the kingdoms of the
nations? Power and might are in Thy hand so
that no one can stand against Thee.

2 CHRONICLES 20:6

When you feel overwhelmed because of the forces that are coming against you, remember what Jehoshaphat did (2 Chronicles 20:6-12). He focused on God, His sovereignty, His power; then he made his request according to the promises of God. This was written for your encouragement. It's an example you can follow today.

REFLECTIONS

Tell God

They reeled and staggered like a drunken man, and were at their wits' end. Then they cried to the LORD in their trouble, and He brought them out of their distresses. He caused the storm to be still, so that the waves of the sea were hushed. Then they were glad because they were quiet; so He guided them to their desired haven.

PSALM 107:27-30

Do you feel threatened? Tell God. Cry to Him. He is never deaf to the cry of His child. Because you are His child and He is your Father, your well-being is His responsibility.

REFLECTIONS

Talk to God

Should evil come upon us, the sword, or judgment, or pestilence, or famine, we will stand...before Thee...and cry to Thee in our distress, and Thou wilt hear and deliver us...O our God, wilt Thou not judge them? For we are powerless before this great multitude who are coming against us; nor do we know what to do, but our eyes are on Thee.

2 Chronicles 20:9,12

In trying times, the best thing we can do is submit to God. Talk aloud to God. Confirm again your desire to serve and follow Him fully. Tell Him that your one and foremost passion is to be found pleasing to Him.

REFLECTIONS

....

....

....

....

....

You're Never Alone

Oh give us help against the adversary,
for deliverance by man is in vain.
Through God we shall do valiantly; and it is
He who will tread down our adversaries.

Psalm 108:12,13

Remember, Beloved, when an adversary comes against you, the adversary is coming against the One who abides in you. You're never alone, you're never without help.

REFLECTIONS

The Lord Will Ambush the Enemy

And when [Jehoshaphat] had consulted with the people, he appointed those who sang to the LORD and those who praised Him in holy attire, as they went out before the army and said, "Give thanks to the LORD, for His lovingkindness is everlasting."

2 CHRONICLES 20:21

Give every situation to your God. Then go forth singing His praises! The Lord will ambush the enemy. You watch. I have seen the reality of this truth many times in my own life and in the lives of others.

REFLECTIONS

True Victory

Submit therefore to God. Resist the devil and he will flee from you.

James 4:7

It's war! The enemy's time is short! Jesus is coming soon! But thanks be to God who always causes us to triumph in *Him*. Remember that true victory is only found in faith's obedience to God's Word. As you go forth to battle, keep bringing every thought captive to Jesus Christ and don't give the devil any place in your mind or in your life.

REFLECTIONS

....

....

....

....

....

The Son of the Living God

He said to them, "But who do you say
that I am?" And Simon Peter answered and
said, "Thou art the Christ, the Son of the living
God." And Jesus answered and said to him,
"Blessed are you, Simon Barjona, because flesh and
blood did not reveal this to you,
but My Father who is in heaven."

MATTHEW 16:15-17

God doesn't run any "Second-Hand Faith Shops."

REFLECTIONS

....

....

....

....

....

243

Your Number-One Priority

He who loves father or mother more than Me is not worthy of Me; and he who loves son or daughter more than Me is not worthy of Me.

MATTHEW 10:37

Never forget, Beloved, your relationship with God is your number-one priority. When you put God where He belongs, it helps you to appropriately deal with every other relationship in a freeing way—and a way pleasing to God. You may not always meet others' expectations, but you will have done what God asks—and that will bring peace to your heart and conscience.

REFLECTIONS

....

....

....

....

....

The Future Is Certain

Surely the Lord G*OD does nothing unless He reveals His secret counsel to His servants the prophets.*

AMOS 3:7

Does it seem like the world is falling apart? Do you wonder where we are headed—how it will all end? Although the future is uncertain to so many, it is not uncertain for believers. It's all recorded in the Book. God doesn't keep His children in the dark. He has a secure future for you, but you'll not be secure in it if you don't know His Book, the Bible. Knowing the Old Testament is fundamental to knowing God and understanding His plans for the future.

REFLECTIONS

....

....

....

....

....

Don't Be Deceived!

And then that lawless one will be revealed whom the Lord will slay with the breath of His mouth...That is, the one whose coming is in accord with the activity of Satan, with all power and signs and false wonders, and with all the deception of wickedness for those who perish, because they did not receive the love of the truth so as to be saved.

2 THESSALONIANS 2:8-10

Events occurring in Europe, the middle East, and Israel are valid indicators that our Lord's coming is near. In the last days there is going to be a great deception and a falling away from the faith. You must learn God's Word so that you won't be deceived!

REFLECTIONS

Build Your Relationships

Let love of the brethren continue. Do not neglect to show hospitality to strangers, for by this some have entertained angels without knowing it. Remember the prisoners, as though in prison with them, and those who are ill-treated, since you yourselves also are in the body.

HEBREWS 13:1-3

One of the major reasons our society is falling apart is that we have neglected interpersonal relationships. We're too busy—even doing good things. Turn off the television and talk to one another. Open your home to others. Build your relationships with family and friends. Remember, people are God's utmost concern.

REFLECTIONS

Invest in the Work of God

Jesus said to him, "If you wish to be complete, go and sell your possessions and give to the poor, and you shall have treasure in heaven; and come, follow me."

MATTHEW 19:21

In light of the Lord's coming, invest in the work of God. Your treasures here are going to be destroyed, so put your money in the Lord's work, which will pay eternal dividends. Concentrate on the necessities rather than the luxuries. I know that may not be as much fun right now, but it will keep you from being ashamed when you see Him face-to-face.

REFLECTIONS

Prepare for the Days Ahead

Prepare to meet your God.

Amos 4:12

The five words in today's Scripture have been ringing in my heart, Beloved. They are pealing from the bell tower of heaven—alerting us to the near coming of the Lord, calling us to repentance and prayer, warning us to prepare for the days ahead.

REFLECTIONS

....

....

....

....

....

Hate Evil; Love Good

Seek good and not evil, that you may live; and thus may the LORD God of hosts be with you, just as you have said! Hate evil, love good, and establish justice in the gate! Perhaps the LORD God of hosts may be gracious to the remnant of Joseph.

AMOS 5:14,15

The Bible tells us that what was written beforehand in the Old Testament was written for our learning and admonition so that through perseverance and encouragement we might have hope (1 Corinthians 10:11, Romans 15:4). The prophet Amos sounds for us a call to repentance, to prayer—a cry from the throne of God through His prophet.

REFLECTIONS

It Is Not Too Late!

For thus says the LORD to the house of Israel,
"Seek Me that you may live."

AMOS 5:4

As God brought His judgments of locusts and fires out of control upon Israel, Amos interceded, and the Word tells us that the Lord changed His mind. It is not too late for us! Earnest prayer uttered from repentant hearts indicates God's justice when He, in mercy, spares His people.

REFLECTIONS

....

....

....

....

....

Never Let Go

He also testified and said, "I have found David the son of Jesse, a man after My heart, who will do all My will."

Acts 13:22

As I've prayed and read in the Psalms, I've noticed the gamut of emotions and situations David had to deal with. And I've seen how, even in his failure and sin, David never let go of God. And when David's life was over, God called him a man after His own heart!

REFLECTIONS

....

....

....

....

....

Knowing God

Come to Me, all who are weary
and heavy-laden, and I will give you rest.

MATTHEW 11:28

Even when I've been weak, to the place of tears, I've found rest. Rest in the promises of our Father, rest in the assurance that nothing depends upon me. It all depends on Him. I'm simply to trust and obey, to be still and know He is God.

REFLECTIONS

....

....

....

....

....

Our Calling

Be still, and know that I am God;
I will be exalted among the nations,
I will be exalted in the earth.

Psalm 46:10 (NIV)

I couldn't do what today's Scripture calls us to if I didn't know my God and His Word. As we make knowing Him and His word our priority and passion, we will be able to rest in faith in the day of testing. And in doing so, we'll please Him—which, above all, is our calling.

REFLECTIONS

Do It!

For what thanks can we render to God for you ...as we night and day keep praying most earnestly that we may see your face, and may complete what is lacking in your faith?

1 Thessalonians 3:9,10

There is a mandate of the church to take those whom God saves and establish them in His Word as that which produces reverence for Him. Ask God who, when, and where—then do it.

REFLECTIONS

.....

.....

.....

.....

.....

❧ 255 ❧

Jesus Is the Head

I am the Lord, *that is My name;*
I will not give My glory to another,
nor My praise to graven images.

Isaiah 42:8

Beloved, don't put people on pedestals. Not one of us is sufficient in and of ourselves. Nor is any part of the body to be exalted—except the head. And Jesus is the head (Ephesians 1:22). Let's love one another, but let's not exalt anyone but Jesus.

REFLECTIONS

Led by the Spirit

Then he answered and said to me,
"This is the word of the LORD to Zerubbabel saying, 'Not by might nor by power, but by My Spirit,' says the LORD of hosts."

ZECHARIAH 4:6

It's time for Christians to be led by the Spirit instead of Madison Avenue. It's time for Christians to start thinking biblically and praying biblically instead of allowing themselves to be manipulated by the schemes of man. Who are we going to follow?

REFLECTIONS

....

....

....

....

....

Be on the Alert

Therefore be on the alert, for you do not know which day your Lord is coming.... For this reason you be ready too; for the Son of Man is coming at an hour when you do not think He will.

Matthew 24:42,44

It's time to serve our Lord. Pray that you'll continue to look to our precious Lord in all things. Pray that you will discern the times and be about His business while there's still time. Pray that you'll know and be established in the Word of God, living it out in a wise and uncompromising way. As you pray, pray these things for the whole body of Christ. The millennium of His coming is surely upon us.

REFLECTIONS

The Critical Difference

How blessed are those who observe His testimonies,
who seek Him with all their heart.

Psalm 119:2

What difference does it make if you're not in the Word of God on a daily basis? It makes a critical difference. It's the difference between a Hi-how-are-You?-By-the-way-I've-been-meaning-to-tell-You relationship with God and a deep intimacy with your heavenly Father.

REFLECTIONS

....

....

....

....

....

Revived Through God's Word

This is my comfort in my affliction,
that Thy word has revived me.

Psalm 119:50

The difference regular reading of God's Word can make in your life is the difference between a panic attack in the unexpected jolts of life and a supernatural peace in the midst of the worst storm. It's the difference between confusion and quiet confidence.

REFLECTIONS

....

....

....

....

....

In the Word

Thy word is a lamp to my feet,
and a light to my path.

PSALM 119:105

Does it make a difference if you're not in the Word of God on a daily basis? All the difference between a restless I-don't-know-what's-missing-but-something-is kind of feeling and a surety that all is well with your soul. It's the difference between running off in a thousand different directions and knowing that this is what you are to do.

REFLECTIONS

....

....

....

....

....

My Refuge

Thou art my hiding place and my shield;
I wait for Thy word.

Psalm 119:114

When you know God and His Word, you know where to run for refuge, you know where to rest your case, you know who has all the facts. And this knowledge eases all the tension as you enter the rest of faith.

REFLECTIONS

....

....

....

....

....

Food for Life

And He humbled you and let you be hungry, and fed you with manna...that He might make you understand that man does not live by bread alone, but man lives by everything that proceeds out of the mouth of the LORD.

DEUTERONOMY 8:3

If you begin to study the Bible on a daily basis and live by what God says, you will soon discover that being in the Word on a daily basis is like gathering manna every day. It is food for life. A moment with God is fine—but it's just a nibble. I long for you to study it precept upon precept, learning the Bible book by book.

REFLECTIONS

The Solution to Every Problem

If Thy law had not been my delight, then I would have perished in my affliction. I will never forget Thy precepts, for by them Thou hast revived me.

PSALM 119:92,93

Do we realize that the solution to every problem, every hurt, every dilemma can be found between the covers of His holy Word—in its precepts, principles, examples, commands, promises, warnings, and teachings? To partake of it daily is to be nourished and made strong—prepared for every situation of life.

REFLECTIONS

Fear the Lord

The fear of the LORD *is the beginning of knowledge.*

PROVERBS 1:7

The word for "fear" in today's Scripture means a reverential trust and awesome respect. If we really respect God for who He is, then we will make listening to Him a priority. If we fear Him, we'll trust what He says and live accordingly, no matter what the situation. Then we'll have His wisdom for every situation of life.

REFLECTIONS

Know God

The LORD favors those who fear Him,
those who wait for His lovingkindness.

PSALM 147:11

When we know God through His Word and through daily intimacy with Him we retain the healthy fear (respect and trust) that God says we are to have of Him. Yet at the same time, that unhealthy dread of what God might do if we submit to Him disappears, for we know His character and comprehend the depth of His love.

REFLECTIONS

The Only Foundation

The Lord GOD is my strength, and He has made my feet like hinds' feet, and makes me walk on my high places.

HABAKKUK 3:19

There is no other foundation than God's Word, Beloved! No other is needed, because the Word of God is totally sufficient. If you will embrace the Word of God and bring every dilemma and lay it at the feet of God's Word, then you'll find yourself, like Habakkuk, walking with hinds' feet and not slipping.

REFLECTIONS

267

It Is Not Easy

If anyone comes to Me, and does not hate his own father and mother and wife and children and brothers and sisters, yes, and even his own life, he cannot be My disciple. Whoever does not carry his own cross and come after Me cannot be My disciple.

LUKE 14:26,27

Have you discovered that following Jesus is not easy? Jesus never indicated that it would be. Throughout His ministry, He reminded His followers there was a cost and that they needed to count it. The rewards will come in the future.

REFLECTIONS

....

....

....

....

....

268

Peace in Jesus

These things I have spoken to you, that in Me you may have peace. In the world you have tribulation, but take courage; I have overcome the world.

John 16:33

O precious child of God, today will not be without temptation, trials, testings, difficulties, and challenges. In this world we will have tribulation. But Jesus does promise us peace—in Him.

REFLECTIONS

Words of Eternal Life

Simon Peter answered Him, "Lord, to whom shall we go? You have words of eternal life."

John 6:68

Only Jesus holds the words of eternal life. They're not words of death, but of life. They're not just for today, but for eternity. He knows our past, our present, our future. He's been there, and He will be there for all of our present and future circumstances.

REFLECTIONS

....

....

....

....

....

Words of Truth

Sanctify them in the truth; Thy word is truth.

John 17:17

The words of eternal life that Jesus offers are words of truth—not lies, like the enemy's. They're the daily bread which nourishes our soul so we can confront and manage each day and all that He allows that day to bring. They set us apart and give us discernment about the issues of life that the world cannot match. We have truth—unadulterated truth.

REFLECTIONS

....

....

....

....

....

❧ 271 ❧

Where Do We Turn?

Jesus said therefore to the twelve, "You do not want to go away also, do you?" Simon Peter answered Him, "Lord, to whom shall we go? You have words of eternal life."

JOHN 6:67,68

All of us face times of incredible warfare in our lives—often on a multitude of fronts. Where do we turn? The only place to turn is to the One who has the words of eternal life!

REFLECTIONS

....

....

....

....

....

Protected by God

I will lift up my eyes to the mountains;
from whence shall my help come?
My help comes from the LORD, *who made heaven*
and earth. He will not allow your foot to slip;
He who keeps you will not slumber.

PSALM 121:1-3

Whenever the children of Israel found themselves in trouble, God always reminded them that He was the one who created this world and all that is in it! If He did that—is there anything He could not do? Of course He could protect them! And He will protect you.

REFLECTIONS

....

....

....

....

....

❧ 273 ❧

His Throne

Thy throne, O God, is forever and ever; a scepter of uprightness is the scepter of Thy kingdom.

PSALM 45:6

The sky may be absolutely black; the wind may be howling; we may be wondering if we will ever get home...yet we can rest in Him. God never leaves His throne.

REFLECTIONS

....

....

....

....

....

The Promises of God

For as many as may be the promises of God, in Him they are yes; wherefore also by Him is our Amen to the glory of God through us.

2 CORINTHIANS 1:20

What do you do when you face "impossible" situations? You can decide there is no way out and run. You can be carried along by what you see, what you hear, what you're experiencing. Or you can choose the only option that comes with a warranty: run to the promises of God!

REFLECTIONS

Cling to God

"For as the waistband clings to the waist of a man, so I made the whole household of Israel and the whole household of Judah cling to Me," declares the LORD, "that they might be for Me a people, for renown, for praise, and for glory."

JEREMIAH 13:11

Wrap yourself around God. If others entice you to doubt Him, to pull away, to let go and do it your way, don't. You'll be ruined. Cling to God no matter what and watch what you'll become.

REFLECTIONS

....

....

....

....

....

Trust God

He only is my rock and my salvation,
my stronghold; I shall not be shaken.
On God my salvation and my glory rest;
the rock of my strength, my refuge is in God.
Trust in Him at all times, O people; pour out your
heart before Him; God is a refuge for us.

PSALM 62:6-8

I don't know what disappointments you have to face, Beloved, but I can tell you with utmost confidence that God is no respecter of persons, only a respecter of faith. Don't give up! Trust God's intentions and His capabilities.

REFLECTIONS

....

....

....

....

....

The Things Above

If then you have been raised up with Christ,
keep seeking the things above...Set your mind
on the things above, not on the things that
are on earth. For you have died and your
life is hidden with Christ in God.

Colossians 3:1-3

If you feel your fervor for God cooling even slightly, carefully examine your thinking and reasoning—your inner man—and carefully examine your activities—your outer man—to see if you have allowed sin to cohabit in your heart. God is a jealous God. He does not want sin in your life.

REFLECTIONS

....

....

....

....

....

Guard Your Heart!

When Christ, who is our life, is revealed, then you also will be revealed with Him in glory. Therefore consider the members of your earthly body as dead to immorality, impurity, passion, evil desire, and greed, which amounts to idolatry. For it is on account of these things that the wrath of God will come.

Colossians 3:4-6

Guard your heart! Immorality, wickedness, greed, and spiritual seduction are on the rise—and they will continue to increase. Those who do not guard their hearts will fall prey to these things, and the aftermath will be bitterness of soul.

REFLECTIONS

....

....

....

....

....

A Way Pleasing to God

Arise, O Lord, in Thine anger;
lift up Thyself against the rage of my adversaries,
and arouse Thyself for me; Thou hast appointed
judgment. And let the assembly of the peoples
encompass Thee; and over them return
Thou on high. The Lord judges the peoples;
vindicate me, O Lord, according to my
righteousness and my integrity that is in me.

Psalm 7:6-8

Rest assured, Beloved, the wicked will not go unjudged. They cannot touch you and escape His punishment. All you need to do is make sure you behave and respond in a way pleasing to God. Retain your integrity. He will vindicate you.

REFLECTIONS

....

....

....

....

....

Under His Wings

He who dwells in the shelter of the Most High will abide in the shadow of the Almighty. I will say to the L*ORD, "My refuge and my fortress, My God, in whom I trust!" ...He will cover you with His pinions, and under His wings you may seek refuge; His faithfulness is a shield and bulwark.*

PSALM 91:1,2,4

Let's not leave the place of our appointment. There under the security of "His wings" we can dwell, knowing that whatever comes our way must first come through Him. He will be our shield.

REFLECTIONS

....

....

....

....

....